THE OPEN
Golf's Oldest Major

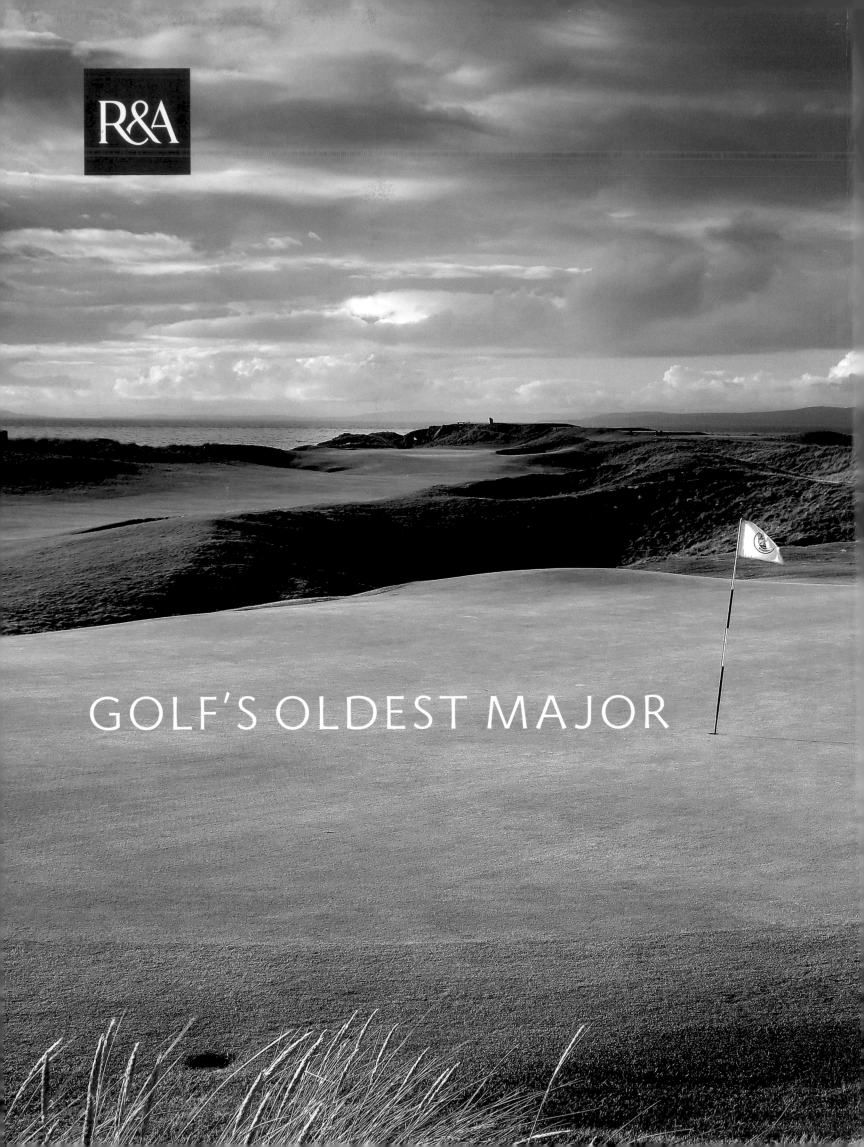

GOLF'S OLDEST MAJOR

Text by Donald Steel   *Foreword by Arnold Palmer*   *Afterword by Peter Dawson*

THE OPEN

RIZZOLI
NEW YORK

New York · Paris · London · Milan

First published in the United States
of America in 2010 by
Rizzoli International Publications, Inc.
300 Park Avenue South
New York, NY 10010

www.rizzoliusa.com

All photography supplied by Getty Images
except images on pp 10, 17, and 20, courtesy
The R&A; pp 40, 44, 134, and 238–239,
courtesy *Golf Illustrated*/Bauer Media;
p 66, courtesy RCAHMS; p 297, courtesy
of Peter Crabtree; and pp 212–213, courtesy
of the Royal Portrush Golf Club.

Editors (for The R&A)
Angela D. Howe
Peter N. Lewis

Photography editors (for Getty Images)
Marc Webbon
Rob Harborne
David Cannon

2010 2011 2012 2013 / 10 9 8 7 6 5 4 3 2 1

Designed by Dalrymple
Printed in Singapore

ISBN-13: 978-0-8478-3308-5
ISBN-10: 0-8478-3308-9

Library of Congress Catalog Control
Number: 2009940781

Frontispiece: The 15th green at Turnberry.

www.opengolf.com

Contents

Foreword

1960 *opposite*

Arnold Palmer during The Open Championship at St Andrews.

2006 *previous pages*

Chris DiMarco celebrates holing a birdie putt on the 13th green during the final round of the 2006 Open Championship at Hoylake.

I played in my first Open Championship fifty years ago at St Andrews. I entered the 1960 Championship primarily because I did not feel that you could ever call yourself a great champion if you didn't play internationally, and particularly in The Open Championship. Growing up, I had read about The Open and many of the players who inspired me, like Bobby Jones, Walter Hagen, and Sam Snead—men who had played in and won The Open, making it clearly one of the world's most important major championships.

When I arrived in St Andrews that year, I was a bit awestruck; it was a totally different panorama than I had ever seen in my life, but one that I grew to enjoy very quickly. St Andrews, the area and the golf course, intrigued me. I thought I could win The Open that year—in fact, I nearly did. But Kel Nagle won, a great champion and a great guy. That spoiled my party, but it still was one of the greatest experiences of my life.

I came back the next year to Royal Birkdale. My second round there in 1961 certainly ranks as one of the best rounds I ever played, considering the conditions, probably the worst I have ever experienced. I went on to win the Claret Jug that week. It fulfilled a lifetime ambition, something that I was determined I had to do before considering myself a good player.

I defended my title at Troon in 1962. The course was dry, as dry in fact as I ever faced in an Open Championship. With those conditions and Troon's saddleback fairways, you had to hit the ball right on line to keep it out of the rough. That made the course even more challenging than it already was. I have always been particularly proud of those four rounds that year at Troon.

After that, many more Americans started to come to the United Kingdom to play in the Open. One of the things that held back the Open and kept it from becoming even more important and successful, though, was the fact that in those days everybody, including the defending champion, had to play in a 36-hole qualifier. After I had finished second, won it twice, and still would have had to qualify, I told the R&A that I wouldn't be coming back in future years under those conditions. Realizing that it was in the best interests of the Championship, the R&A then modified its qualifying requirements to ensure that the world's best players would enter and play in the Championship.

I know I did the right thing when I first went to St Andrews in 1960. My subsequent success seemed to have spurred on the influx of America's leading players in the years that followed, validating The Open's status among the game's major championships. I hope that I have had an impact on The Open Championship. That would be a very proud moment in my life.

ARNOLD PALMER

The Claret Jug—or, to use its proper name, The Golf Champion Trophy—was first presented in 1873, thirteen years after the tournament began. The original prize was the Challenge Belt, an ornate belt of red Moroccan leather with a silver buckle. According to the rules of the competition, the Belt would become "the property of the winner by being won three years in succession." In 1870, Tommy Morris Jr. completed a trio of victories and gained possession of the Belt.

As there was no longer a trophy, The Open was not played in 1871. The following year, the R&A, along with the Honourable Company of Edinburgh Golfers and Prestwick Golf Club, agreed to contribute toward the cost of a new trophy and to host the Championship in rotation between them.

There was not enough time to commission the trophy before the 1872 Open, so the winner, again Tommy Morris Jr., was given a medal instead.

The Claret Jug, which was made by Mackay Cunningham & Company of Edinburgh, is hallmarked 1873 and was presented to Tom Kidd following his victory that year at St Andrews. In recognition of his victory in 1872, Tommy Morris' name was the first to be engraved on the Claret Jug.

Introduction

By the simple expedient of being the world's oldest championship, The Open needs only the definite article to mark its identity. Its integrity, importance, and influence are indisputable. Champion Golfer of the Year is a title possessing an enviable resonance, the peak of endeavour and achievement. One glance at the plinth of the celebrated Claret Jug reveals that hardly a legendary name is missing from its roll of honour, a pre-eminence based on the fact that, more than any other championship, it has attracted international fields even in the days when travel was a substantial undertaking.

At the forefront every year is the quest to be the best. The Open has provided the stage for many to take a stride or two along the rocky road to immortality. However, The Open has another unrivalled claim. Its enduring legacy is founded on an insistence that its staging grounds are the traditional links courses unique to the British Isles. Individual venues have fallen in and out of favour but there is still a widely held belief that links golf, and the weather's fickle moods, stretches hearts, nerves, and minds in a manner that makes it the supreme test.

Unlike playing any other type of course, links golf is an adventure—ever changing, never ending, predictable only in its unpredictability. It underlines the cerebral emphasis of the game, rewarding disciplined thought, resilience, patience, and the whole gamut of shot-making. Reading situations correctly, and acting upon them, is the hallmark of champions, the ability to visualise shots a stronger ally than blind reliance on pre-measured distances.

Was a more reassuring commendation ever echoed than that of Tiger Woods after winning at Hoylake in 2006? "The fast conditions enabled every player to be creative. It is how golf used to be played and how it should be played now." Saying the same thing in a different way almost fifty years earlier, Bobby Jones reflected, "Although I did not feel this way in the beginning, I am happy now that I did not miss playing seaside golf when the greens were hard and un-watered and the fairways and putting surfaces like glass. Nothing resulting from man-made design can equal the testing qualities of such conditions."

In one hundred and fifty years, The Open has been through many meta-morphoses, contradiction of the belief that what is seen today is how things have always been. What has sustained it from one generation to the next is the overwhelming feeling that victory represents the most coveted title in golf. Comparisons of the generations, on the other hand, are more difficult. Champions are products of their time, and times change, but The Open has flourished on rivalry—rivalry that, for all its fierceness, is underpinned by the code of etiquette and behaviour that it helped foster. As J. H. Taylor remarked so pertinently long ago, "always remember that however good you may be, the game is your master."

Looking at the full panoply of a modern Open, it is hard to imagine its humble beginnings at Prestwick in 1860. Only a few look back as a reminder of how different the scene was then. Similarly, it would have been fun and fanciful if the first generation of pioneering professionals could have fast-forwarded their remote control buttons to fathom the sophistications of the modern game and the wealth that drives it.

Today, an agent for Young Tom Morris would rub his hands together at the prospect of managing a seventeen-year-old who had just deposed his father as champion—although history doesn't reveal whether Old Tom felt proud or humbled. In a tragically short life, Young Tom was the game's first truly great player, but could Tiger Woods or Padraig Harrington conceive how he performed his miracles, or come to terms with the lack of instant recognition worldwide?

Apart from the more rough and ready condition of Prestwick's 12-hole course, and equipment that was much harder to handle, members of the club were more inclined to wager among themselves than go out and watch. There were no specialist writers to interview the players, no television to spread news far and wide. Indeed, the players had no access to the clubhouse, a circumstance that gave rise to a humorous remark by Herbert Warren Wind, the illustrious American writer on golf. Watching a championship in the 1970s when the epithet "leader in the clubhouse" had become adopted universally, he observed quizzically, "I wonder who the leader in the clubhouse was before the leaders were allowed in the clubhouse."

Walter Hagen declined to enter the clubhouse for one presentation on the grounds that none of the professionals had been allowed near it during the week but, as this photographic catalogue of contrast and comparison illustrates, a century and a half has been as much social study and sartorial sideshow as sporting spectacle.

The role of professional golfer was shaped before The Open's launching in 1860 but The Open undoubtedly helped advance the professional's status first to a level of tolerance, then respectability, and finally all-engulfing stardom. Hagen's significance went far beyond his playing exploits for he was the self-appointed standard-bearer, the first to demand that all players be treated as equals. Young men still use golf to elevate their lives to a level of prosperity to which no other career would lift them and, even if it is true that competitive fall-out is greater now, there is solace that comfortable livings are possible without scaling the heights.

Even in Scotland in 1860, there were relatively few clubs—hence little employment. Travel was far from easy; a journey from Prestwick to St Andrews taking longer than a transatlantic hop by a twenty-first-century golfer in his private plane. Older generations are inured with stoicism, always maintaining they were happy with their lot but the glamour years were still a way off.

Horace Hutchinson, captain of the R&A in 1908 and Amateur champion in 1886 and 1887, added clarity in the Badminton Library: "One can divide into three classes those who derive a precarious subsistence from the game of golf: professional club-makers, professional players who eke out existence by work in the club-maker's shops, and professional caddies, who would be professional players if they played well enough."

In the days to which Hutchinson referred, many professional golfers, like Old Tom Morris, were "keepers of the green" as well. Their duties encompassed organising maintenance, controlling caddies and tending to the needs of members through playing, teaching, and carrying out repairs.

One of the first to concentrate almost solely on the playing side was Young Tom, whose abundant talent meant the links saw far more of him than the family shop did, but most of the home professionals who played in The Open had club affiliations that divided their time. In his book *Taylor on Golf*, J. H. Taylor remarked that it cost a player £10 in expenses to compete in The Open with only the first three prizes worth winning.

Nevertheless, when talk of a strike surfaced in 1899 to pursue an increase in prize money, Taylor was one who opposed the idea even if, during the championship, the first prize was raised to £50. Players' loyalty to their clubs was a state of

Sunrise over a grandstand at Turnberry, as the first day of the 2009 Open Championship dawns; a member of the ground staff prepares the course.

affairs that prevailed until the development of the European Tour in the 1970s, with Peter Thomson making a telling point at the gathering of champions at St Andrews in 2000: "In the 1950s, I was a sort of lone ranger. Every British player was actually a club professional. They had other duties and other worries. They didn't rely on winning prize money to keep the wolf from the door. They had a different attitude come the championships. I must have been more ready, hungrier, I suppose, is the word."

Motivation was a powerful force but, without Thomson's affinity with links-style golf, it would undoubtedly have counted for less. His upbringing on the great courses of Melbourne's Sandbelt was the finest grounding he could have had. No city in the world has more excellent courses within such easy reach and they instilled in him an instinctive love of hard and fast conditions. In a foreword for *Classic Golf Links of Great Britain and Ireland*, he wrote, "The thrill of squeezing a ball against the firm turf, trying to keep it low into the buffeting wind, is something that lingers in the mind forever. It reminds me that a good deal of golf is played along the ground or should be."

To the generation of British golfers growing up in the 1950s, Thomson was the epitome of these traditional virtues. He came to Britain to prove his worth because he knew there was no better place and his loyalty has been unwavering. Before the advent of Arnold Palmer and Jack Nicklaus, his pioneering efforts along with Bobby Locke and Gary Player were uniquely multi-faceted. After a gruelling round in The Open, he would find a seat in a crowded Press Tent and file his own version of events to his waiting newspaper back home. Later, he would join the television commentary team for an hour or two.

His ardent campaigning on a number of issues also stimulated valuable thought but it was his part in expanding an international cast for The Open that was the real benefit. Arnaud Massy led the way in the early 1900s and later Walter Hagen, Bobby Jones, and Gene Sarazen seized the baton and ran with it. Although a visit from America in the 1920s occupied a good three weeks, twelve American victories out of thirteen from 1921 were ample confirmation of the shift of power. Another way of looking at it is that there were only nineteen British and Irish successes between 1920 and 2009, but Palmer's first appearance in 1960 was necessary in drawing renewed attention to the cause.

In his early days as Secretary of the R&A, Keith Mackenzie used a week at the Masters as an annual recruitment drive for The Open, but gradually the message required less amplification. Allied to a growing consciousness of the lure of The Open was the increasing care and attention extended to the players and to the paying public whose welfare was of paramount importance. Value for money was measured in the variety of facilities provided for their enjoyment. Apart from improved catering in the general vicinity of what quickly became known as the Tented Village, grandstands and an up-to-the-minute scoring system were guarantees that everyone knew more and more about what was going on.

Claims about The Open setting trends are accurate and deserved but, in assessing the current role of the R&A whose greatest contribution is seen as their presentation and promotion of The Open, two facts may surprise. The R&A took sole responsibility for its running only from 1920 and was not the instigator of the oldest championship. The Seniors Open Amateur Championship in 1968 was the first championship the R&A conceived, planned, and launched themselves. The Open, The Amateur, and the Boys were all "inherited" from other clubs or individuals.

Looking at the contemporary scene, the R&A's planning is complex and never-ending. From the days when the Secretary used to arrive on the eve of play

2009

4.25 a.m. on day one of the 2009 Open Championship.

with a pot of paint, a length of rope, and call for a few volunteers, they now work years ahead. Their involvement has grown and grown but it wouldn't work half as efficiently without the voluntary contribution of The R&A's Championship Committee members together with those of the Rules of Golf Committee.

It was many years before the Rules of Golf Committee, formed in 1897, justified the need for qualified officials but adjudication is inevitably less frenetic in golf than the spur-of-the-moment decisions essential in faster moving sports. Golf used to be more self-policing but, with so much riding on one decision, golfers became ever more reliant on independent officials who, in turn, are subjected to rigorous examinations in order to prove their worthiness for the task.

A preference for an official to accompany as many matches as possible is a side of the administration that has had to keep pace with the rapid development everywhere but the other surprise is the now unthinkable suggestion floated in 1947, that "The Open Championship be advertised and sold to the highest bidder", although the happy sequel is that it was dismissed without further mention, as was a proposal from the Finance Committee to the Championship Committee that future Opens be confined to links with a large surrounding population. Making a profit from The Open was always a struggle but Ben Hogan's arrival at Carnoustie in 1953 was emphatic evidence of just how much of a box office draw star performers can be.

Gerald Micklem, whose part in the development of The Open over a period of twenty years was immense, went straight to the point, as he always did, in a reflective interview in 1969. He referred to 1953 as a tremendous occasion when people came from everywhere to watch. "That really started everything, got the thing moving the right way. We also made some money. It was a sort of vicious circle in that we never had enough money to spend to entice the good people in order for the R&A to get more money. One was always hesitant about spending money we hadn't got. In 1953, we had money in hand and were able to go ahead."

The 27,069 paying members of the public in 1953 is well below the daily attendance figure expected nowadays at The Open but, in Hogan's day, crowds had to fend for themselves and, with the exception of a few regular stalwarts, would have been more locally based. Plans for the Tay and Forth road bridges had barely reached the drawing board.

Another colossal contribution to the transformation that evolved has been the television coverage and the mellifluous tones at home of Henry Longhurst and Peter Alliss. It thrust The Open onto a world stage, boosting its eminence as well as its bank balance. As a result, substantial operating profits ensure the R&A can distribute largesse to various deserving bodies in various corners of the world.

However, the attraction of looking back over 150 years is not to sing the praises of all things modern. In more limited circumstances, the work of a few provided a continuity that was vital. Pick of the pack must be Bernard Darwin, without whose incomparable writing The Open's records would be, if not blank, much less complete. The current school of writers may give thanks to computers, mobile phones, instant press releases, incessant interviews, intricate scoring systems, and air-conditioned working quarters. Darwin, if he was lucky, had to find a chair in the corner of a noisy clubhouse bar, gather his wits about him, and assemble his imperishable narrative on a few sheets of paper with a nib pen.

This followed long stints watching and gathering information, often in unfriendly weather.

In *Golf Between Two Wars*, one of the most valuable books in the golfing library, he recounted of a Ladies' Championship, "I cannot remember watching on a more unpleasant day, and when at last at a late hour I had completed my account

of the match on partially sopped pieces of paper it never reached London. Yet as a spectacle it was well worth the wetting."

Deciphering Darwin's spidery handwriting became an art form amongst sub-editors and cable offices but the message couldn't have been clearer. Darwin wouldn't have exchanged his method of working for a laptop or a flurry of quotes but, until radio broadcasting and television became more sophisticated, The Open relied largely on newspapers to spread the word.

Here, they have been wonderfully well served by a whole host of writers to whom enormous credit is due for their efforts in promoting The Open's prominence. Of all the sports, the quality of writing about golf has been unmatched, although the expansion of their working premises has been a further phenomenon of championship week. It is nothing now for the Media Centre to have in the region of 750 accredited occupants.

As recently as 1964, a classroom blackboard in a small tent for fifteen or twenty situated on a grassy slope behind the 18th green at St Andrews was adequate for the entire press corps but, in a playing context, it was a week of irrevocable change. Tony Lema, flying in from the States and allowing himself a day and a half to acquaint himself with the Old Course, won in a canter to the accompaniment of his manager conveying the image of a champagne lifestyle. It may have been what is known as shrewd PR but the current crop of young players would regard such publicity as portraying a misleading picture.

One of golf's advantages over most sports is that, for a game conducted at a leisurely pace, you don't have to be a young, highly trained athlete to play it acceptably—or that used to be the belief. Photos of Old Tom, who played in The Open aged sevety-four, scarcely suggest a sprightly halfback; nor do those of Walter Hagen suggest a man unlikely to waste the cocktail hour hitting balls on the range. Harry Vardon's pipe was as much his trademark as the grooved swing he made famous, and Ben Hogan's flick of his cigarette to the ground as he selected a club, an unmistakable part of his pre-shot routine.

Enjoying a drink with your opponent after a round even in The Open is no longer the unwritten rule it used to be. Making tactical and technical adjustments with coaches, or giving a round of interviews, are now greater priority but, in the early years, supposedly less fit golfers thought nothing of deciding The Open over 36 holes in a single day wearing hob-nailed boots, shirt, tie, and heavy tweeds with no access to protective clothing, clubhouse, physiotherapists, or mental gurus, and nowhere to practice.

From the seemingly restrictive Norfolk jacket era through the age of plus fours to the freedom of tailored shirts with sponsored logos, players have become more dress-conscious. Again, Hagen set the standards, although his most intriguing habit was wearing a smart overcoat for the prize giving.

The Challenge Belt, the original Open Championship prize from 1860 until 1870, when it was won outright by Tommy Morris Jr.

Henry Cotton, an obvious disciple, followed his example in 1934, but Sam Snead chose to wear one of his celebrated hats when he received the trophy in 1946. Kel Nagle borrowed a jacket from Peter Thomson to accept his prize in 1960 before greater informality took over, although increased demands on a winner's time means he can hardly draw breath in advance of a presentation ceremony beamed to all corners of the globe.

Not that there is ever any complaint. Thousands would readily have changed places with the winners over a century and a half. Odes of joy are deafened by tales of woe. Doug Sanders, Jean van de Velde, and Tom Watson may contradict the theory that nobody remembers who finishes, second but their public agony was compounded and prolonged by defeat in a play-off.

Play-off is not a popular word among writers, broadcasters, and organisers but the fairly recently curtailed version over 4 holes has won support from onlookers who don't like to go home without hailing the champion. Play-offs were of 36-hole duration until 1963, even if there were only nine in total during that time. They then became 18 holes, of which there were just two, but an interesting statistic is that, up to and including 2009, there have been nineteen play-offs in 138 Open Championships against thirty-three play-offs in 109 US Opens. Coincidentally, from 1995 to 2009, The Open had seven play-offs, the US Open two.

As many ways of winning The Open have been found as there have been champions. In 1888, Jack Burns failed to permit a start at St Andrews of 5, 5, 6, 5, 7, 6 to stand in his way of eventual success. Maybe it inspired him. So, what qualities do Open champions share? The mechanics of hitting the ball together with a high degree of fitness are only part of the equation. Many golfers have mastered the art of developing a repeating swing that commands a whole range of fine shots only to find it deserts them when their needs are greatest.

Greatness is finding the solution when it matters most and holding at bay gremlins that disrupt the clear thinking requisite to preserving judgement and rhythm. The prospect of victory must also be a spur and not a deterrent.

How champions package these ideals has made The Open such a fascinating study but The Open itself can take credit for providing the stimulus that has so often contained magical remedial powers. In 1934, Henry Cotton was ready for the fray—or should have been. He arrived at Sandwich with 4 sets of clubs and, as Henry Longhurst wrote afterwards, "couldn't hit his hat with any of them." Downcast, Cotton decided to "get away altogether," his vow taking the form of caddying for his wife, Toots, in a private match.

A day or two later, he had signed successive cards of 66, 67, 65—fine scores now but unheard of then. A further day later, he was Open champion in spite of a hiccup in the last round which he attributed to something he ate for lunch but, after the celebrations had subsided, he reflected in print, "I feel very much like a medical student or any other person who has passed an exam. That person is just as clever some months before that exam as he is immediately afterwards. But once he has passed that exam, he is qualified."

On that basis, prize giving should be a graduation ceremony. However, the other signal the tale conveys is that half the art of winning championships surrounds the knack of relaxing and escaping from the task at hand. Diversion is sometimes more therapeutic than devotion.

DONALD STEEL

ST ANDREWS

St Andrews

Course length 2005 Open
7,279 yards, par 72

1873 / 1876 / 1879 / 1882 / 1885 / 1888
1891 / 1895 / 1900 / 1905 / 1910 / 1921
1927 / 1933 / 1939 / 1946 / 1955 / 1957
1960 / 1964 / 1970 / 1978 / 1984 / 1990
1995 / 2000 / 2005

Most golfers' idea of heaven is an Open at St Andrews. For the players, there is certainly nothing to compare with victory over the Old Course—Jack Nicklaus maintains that "if you want to be remembered, you have to win at St Andrews." There have been suggestions that every Open Championship should be held there so it is no surprise that it has housed more than any other venue. It is no surprise either that, of the three original courses used for The Open, it is the sole survivor. Recently, it has played host every fifth year.

No course is more public than the Old in the sense that so much is visible of the start and finish from adjacent streets and buildings. The 18th green gives the feeling of being part of the town and, at the climax of an Open, is overlooked by thousands who have paid and a good few hundred who haven't. Necks are strained from many a window. In the playing sense, it is the course of double fairways, double greens, pot bunkers, and the Road Hole—the most infamous in the world, a combination that golf course architects regard as the blueprint of their art for all students to follow and revere. Not that everyone has stood in awe.

Harry Vardon claimed that the Old is "a good course, but its bunkers are badly placed," which may explain why none of his six Open victories took place there. George Duncan, on the other hand, remarked, "What I like about the Old Course, is that you play a very good shot and find yourself in a very bad place." Tiger Woods's reaction in 2000 was to avoid the bunkers altogether in all four rounds, a forerunner to victory by eight strokes that equalled St Andrews' biggest winning margin by J. H. Taylor exactly a hundred years earlier.

Taylor and Woods share with Jack Nicklaus, James Braid and Bob Martin the honour of winning two Opens over the Old Course but two other memories stand out. St Andrews marked the first and last appearances of Arnold Palmer and the victory in 1964 of Tony Lema, with Palmer's caddie on loan—one of the most remarkable of all.

1970 *opposite*
Jack Nicklaus ducks to avoid his putter, which he has thrown in the air in celebration after beating Doug Sanders in the play-off.

previous pages
Daybreak over the Old Course.

previous pages

A view toward the green on the 15th hole.

1984 *above*

Victory fades from Tom Watson's grasp after a misjudged approach to the 17th green ends in a dropped shot. Ahead at the 18th, Seve Ballesteros holed in three, giving him the advantage over Watson, who needed but failed to make an eagle at the 18th.

1984 *right*

Seve Ballesteros' memorable emotional display as he captures his second Open title.

A joyous Costantino Rocca falls to his knees after holing a birdie putt on the 18th to force a play-off with John Daly.

2005

Jose Maria Olazabal gestures theatrically
following his spectacular eagle putt on the
18th during the second round.

1957
Bobby Locke lines up his
Championship-winning putt at
the 72nd hole.

1970

Doug Sanders and his ill-fated
downhill putt for the title. He
missed, forcing a play-off with Jack
Nicklaus, which Nicklaus won.

2000

Jean Van de Velde plays out of the Road Bunker
at the 17th during his second round.

2000

Jose Manuel Carriles attempts to find his way out of Cottage Bunker.

above and right

A familiar feature of the Old Course, the Swilcan Bridge is crossed by spectators in 1905 and competitors in 2005.

following pages

Aerial view of the historic links and town of St Andrews.

1910

Crowds look on as James Braid is presented
with the Jubilee Medal, which was struck to
commemorate the 50th anniversary of The
Open Championship. This was Braid's fifth
and final Open victory and his second win
at St Andrews.

1927
Eager spectators gather round the scoreboard.

1927 *top*
A relaxed Bobby Jones talks to Jim
Alexander, the Old Course starter.

1970 *above*
Doug Sanders relaxes with spectators before
the play-off with Jack Nicklaus.

1970 *opposite*
The mood is tense as Nicklaus and Sanders go head
to head in the play-off.

1970 *following pages*
Flooding caused by a thunderstorm on the first day
of the Championship forces play to be suspended.

1990 *previous pages*

The sun shines for Nick Faldo as he continues to head the field on day three.

opposite

A view of the green on the 5th hole.

1964 *above right*

Tony Lema, the 1964 Open Champion.

1955 *right*

Peter Thomson, on his way to winning a second Open title. His victory the following year made him the first hat-trick champion since The Open was played over 72 holes. No player had achieved three consecutive wins since Bob Ferguson in 1882.

1978 *following pages*

Jack Nicklaus on the verge of victory.

1957 *opposite above*

Bobby Locke practices before the start of the
Championship, which he went on to win.

1990 *opposite below*

Payne Stewart prepares to hit his tee shot at
the 18th hole on the third day. He finished
the Championship tied for second place.

1927 *above*

Bobby Jones tees off at the 1st hole of The
Open. He won the Championship that year
by six strokes.

2005 *above and left*

Tiger Woods faces the world's cameras after his victory at the 2005 Open Championship.

2005 *following pages*

Jack Nicklaus acknowledges the crowd after completing his second round. His challenge ended there, as did his Open Championship career. It was an emotional final farewell for the three-time champion.

2005

A huge crowd surrounds the 18th green to watch Tiger Woods deliver another winning performance.

MUSSELBURGH

MUSSELBURGH ⑤ OPEN CHAMPIONS

BOB FERGUSON
1880 1881 1882

MUNGO PARK
1874

WILLIE PARK SNR
1860 1863 1866 1875

WILLIE PARK JNR
1887 1889

DAVID BROWN
1886

THIS PLAQUE ALSO HONOURS TWO FURTHER GREAT MUSSELBURGH GOLFERS · WILLIE DUNN JR. FIRST UNOFFICIAL US OPEN CHAMPION AND WILLIE CAMPBELL FIRST PROFESSIONAL BROOKLINE COUNTY CLUB MASSACHUSETTS

Musselburgh

Musselburgh played a relatively short but significant role in the development of The Open. In conjunction with Prestwick and St Andrews, it formed the rota of courses on which the Championship was played between 1872 and 1891, a period that saw a substantial increase in the size of fields—making the game more popular and competitive. Many contestants were Musselburgh golfers, the first six home in 1880 all being local players. The Park family and Bob Ferguson were its most notable citizens.

The nine-hole Musselburgh course had been the adopted home of the Honourable Company of Edinburgh Golfers since 1836, when the development of the historic Leith Links forced them to move from the city. In 1891, they found a new home further down the coast at Muirfield, a move that signalled Musselburgh's championship demise—although nine holes for The Open wouldn't have been suitable for much longer. However, the existing nine holes, in and around the racecourse, remain as a reminder of its glory days.

Course length 19th century
3,000 yards

1874 / 1877 / 1880 / 1883 / 1886 / 1889

opposite above

The five locally-born winners of Open Championships held at Musselburgh are commemorated on a plaque set into the exterior wall of what is now the clubhouse of the Musselburgh Old Course Golf Club.

opposite below

Aerial view of the Musselburgh links and the surrounding racecourse.

previous pages

The 1st hole at Musselburgh with the racecourse grandstand in the background.

MUIRFIELD

Muirfield

Course length 2002 Open
7,034 yards, par 71

1892 / 1896 / 1901 / 1906 / 1912
1929 / 1935 / 1948 / 1959 / 1966
1972 / 1980 / 1987 / 1992 / 2002

Nobody, except the members, would complain if every Open were played at Muirfield. It is top of many a player's hit parade largely because of its essential fairness, but two of its champions expressed their affection more lastingly. James Braid named his second son Harry Muirfield Braid and Jack Nicklaus his prized creation in Ohio, Muirfield Village. It comes as no surprise, therefore, that Nicklaus believes, "Muirfield is my favourite course, to me the best on the Open Championship rota."

Architecturally, it offers the perfect formula of an anti-clockwise inward half cocooned in a clockwise outward nine, although the patent belongs to a combination of minds. It allows spectators easy freedom in moving from match to match, at the same time keeping players constantly studying wind patterns as holes change direction. Certainly, no course had more immediate recognition. Brought into play in 1891, it held its first Open the following year, a triumph in his first Open for the amateur Harold Hilton.

Hilton's last two rounds of 72 and 74 were amazingly low for those days but Muirfield quickly built up a distinguished array of champions. Vardon, Braid (twice), and Ray represent the pride of the old-timers. Hagen completed his fourth and Cotton his third victory over the links. Player, Nicklaus, Trevino, Watson, Faldo (twice), and Els are a handsome pick of the modern era, leaving Alf Perry in 1935 as something of the odd man out—but anyone hitting a wooden club out of a bunker onto the 14th green, finding the 18th green with another spoon shot from the fairway, and leaving the field four shots behind deserves his place among the galaxy of stars.

More recent memories surround Nicklaus's 3-iron and Faldo's 5-iron second shots on the 72nd hole that sealed their first Open victories in 1966 and 1987 respectively, and an exquisite bunker shot by Ernie Els to finally shake off his pursuers in The Open's first four-man play-off in 2002.

1992 *opposite*
John Cook shows his frustration after missing an eagle putt at the 5th hole in the third round.

previous pages
The green at the 18th hole, with the clubhouse in the background.

1987

Nick Faldo's winning putt. This was his first
Open victory. He would go on to win at
St Andrews in 1990 and at Muirfield again
in 1992.

1992

Nick Faldo on the 5th tee during the final
round of the Championship. It was the title
he almost gave away to John Cook, having
secured a comfortable four-stroke lead
with only nine holes to play. Falling to two
behind, he re-mounted his challenge over
the last four holes to win by a single stroke.

1929 *opposite above*

Walter Hagen and Henry Cotton
accompanied by their caddies.

1929 *above*

Smartly dressed spectators follow play.

1948 *opposite below*

King George VI (far right) joins
the spectators.

following pages

Looking down toward the 10th green with
the hills of Fife visible in the background
across the Firth of Forth.

1966

Arnold Palmer looks on as Gary Player takes
a swing on the practice ground.

1966 *right and below*

Jack Nicklaus finds himself in trouble under the main stand at the 18th during the first round of the Championship. Despite this, he finished the day as joint leader with Jimmy Hitchcock. Nicklaus was in the lead after the second round, but dropped to second place, behind Phil Rogers, during the third. He went on to win by a single stroke from Doug Sanders and Dave Thomas.

2002 *above and opposite*

A storm hit Muirfield on the third day of
the Championship, causing the scores to
skyrocket. Among those caught in the worst
of the weather were Colin Montgomerie and
Tiger Woods.

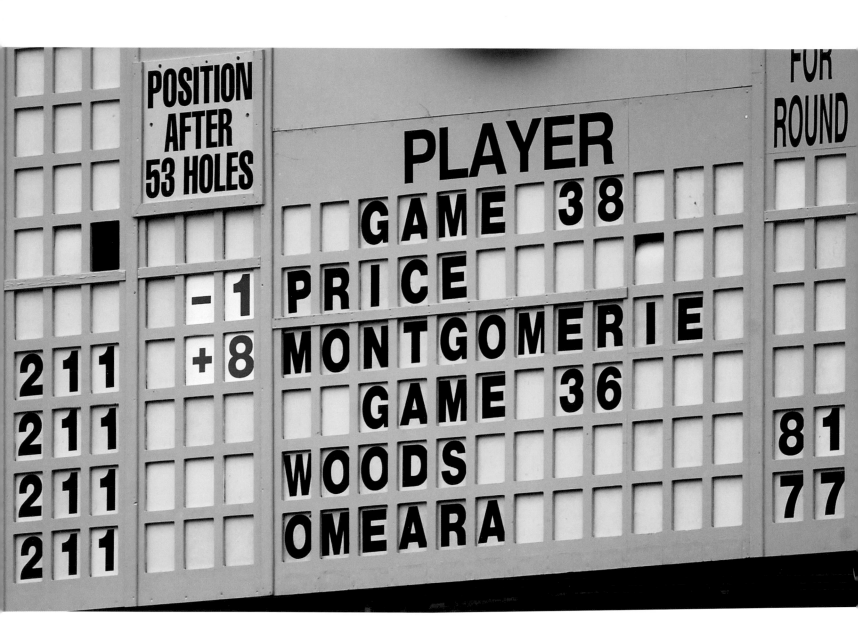

2002

Ernie Els plays a magnificent shot out of the bunker onto the 13th green during the final round.

2002 *above and middle*

After one of the most dramatic finishes in Open Championship history, a victorious Ernie Els is lifted up by Thomas Levet and (*middle*) throws his cap in the air in celebration. Els defeated Levet in a sudden death play-off after they finished level in the 4-hole play-off, which was contested between Els, Levet, Stuart Appleby, and Steve Elkington.

2002 *above*

Thomas Levet celebrates his eagle on the 17th green during the final round of the Championship.

1980 *following pages*

Tom Watson enjoys the moment as he wins his third Open Championship title.

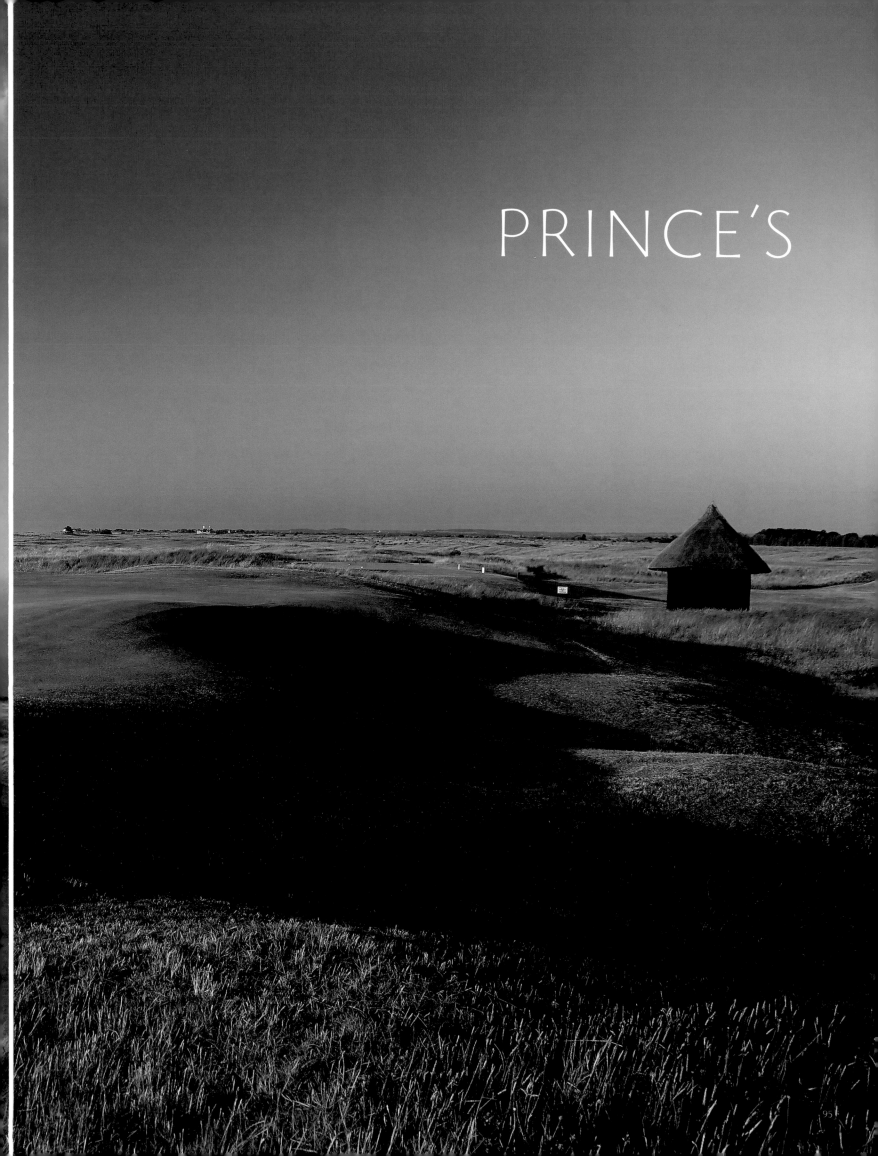

PRINCE'S

Royal St George's

Course length 2003 Open
7,106 yards, par 71

1894 / 1899 / 1904 / 1911 / 1922
1928 / 1934 / 1938 / 1949 / 1981
1985 / 1993 / 2003

The Open's association with Royal St George's, informally known as Sandwich, has been as chequered and controversial as any. In its earliest days, a chorus of complaint that it was "a one-shot" course led to a number of changes although Bernard Darwin, who exchanged the law for writing golf, could always be relied upon to act as Counsel for the Defence. He called it "perfect bliss."

Sadly no Open was held at the club during Darwin's presidency between 1952 and 1961. For a number of reasons, a long period of isolation followed the 1949 Open. However, several solutions, including new 3rd, 8th, and 11th holes, led to its welcome recall in 1981.

For many professionals, playing Royal St George's was their first acquaintance with a course with a definite air of spaciousness, although its characteristic sand hills give each hole a separate identity. It demands controlled driving to fairways with distinctive humps and hollows followed by an attractive variety of second shots to interesting greens that conform to no particular style.

As befits the title of a club bearing the name of England's patron saint, English professionals have found it more to their liking than other Open courses. Its first Open, in 1894, produced the first victory by an English professional, J. H. Taylor. Henry Cotton rewrote the records in 1934, thereby ending a period of eleven years without a British victory, and, in 1985, Sandy Lyle, who played amateur golf for England, was the first British champion since Tony Jacklin in 1969.

Harry Vardon paid the course the compliment of winning twice. Jack White, Sunningdale's first club professional, was the first winner to break 70 in the final round in 1904 and Reg Whitcombe rode the terrible storm more successfully than any in 1938.

A counter to that domestic pattern was seen in the hard-to-predict victories of the Americans, Bill Rogers (1981) and Ben Curtis (2003). Truer to form was the play-off success of Bobby Locke against Harry Bradshaw in 1949 but, to endorse Sandwich's international appeal, Walter Hagen emulated Vardon by winning twice in 1922 and 1928. However, for sustained brilliance, nothing exceeded Greg Norman in 1993. His total of 267 is the lowest on record. He is one of three champions to have completed four rounds under 70 and the champion with the lowest final round (64).

1981 *opposite*
Jack Nicklaus and Seve Ballesteros find their focus on the practice green prior to the start of the Championship.

previous pages
View of the 6th hole, 'The Maiden,' flanked by bunkers, with Sandwich Bay in the background.

1985

Sandy Lyle celebrates his Open victory.
He was the first British winner since
Tony Jacklin in 1969.

1993 *following pages*

Bernhard Langer and Greg Norman walk
down the fairway of the 18th hole during
the final round.

2003 *left*

Thomas Bjorn sees his Championship lead disappear when he takes three shots to get out of the bunker by the 16th green.

2003 *right*

Ben Curtis sinks his putt at the last hole, but does not yet know that it has won him the Championship.

1928 & 2003
Media interest then and now: Walter Hagen
(*this page*) and Ben Curtis (*opposite*).

1934 *opposite*

Henry Cotton putts on the 6th green on the way to his first Open victory.

1949 *left*

Players in action on the 6th green during the Championship.

2003 *below*

Tiger Woods putting on the 6th green during the final round.

1993 *opposite*

Greg Norman hits out of the rough during the second round.

1993 *above*

Nick Faldo plays an approach shot out of light rough during the third round.

1981 *following pages*

Bill Rogers hugs his caddie after winning the Championship with a total of 276, four strokes clear of the runner-up, Bernhard Langer.

1949 *opposite above*

Bobby Locke drives from the 18th tee.

1981 *opposite below*

Greg Norman escapes from the rough during a practice round before the Championship begins.

2003 *following pages*

The large bunkers down the right side of the 4th hole.

1922 *top*

There is a relaxed atmosphere on the course, as a young family watches from the side of the tee.

1934 *above*

Henry Cotton drives off, watched by Charles Whitcombe.

1934

Henry Cotton signs autographs for fans after
winning the first of his three Open titles.

1928

Walter Hagen is applauded by Edward, Prince of Wales (later King Edward VIII), as he prepares to accept the Claret Jug for the third time. His fourth and final victory came at Muirfield the following year.

1949 *above*

A cluster of spectators, eager for an update, gather around the BBC radio broadcasting booth.

2003 *opposite*

All eyes on Tiger Woods as he tees off for his final round.

ROYAL CINQUE PORTS

Royal Cinque Ports

Course length 1920 Open
6,575 yards

1909 / 1920

Deal staged two Opens and very nearly three others. It was scheduled to hold the 1915 Open which was cancelled owing to World War I. It was also supposed to hold the 1938 Open but withdrew on 7 May 1938 on account of extensive storm damage suffered by the course. The invitation for the 1949 championship was not made until May 1948, but the lack of financial help from the R&A for work to improve course conditions after the terrible floods of 1947 led to Royal St George's taking over in 1949, as they had in 1938. Deal, therefore, holds the dubious distinction of having had more Opens cancelled than played.

Nevertheless, Deal's adoption to the rota was no more than it deserved. Its playing merit has never been in question. Bernard Darwin, in fact, thought it the "most testing and severe" of all the championship courses.

In 1909, The Open was dominated by J. H. Taylor and James Braid, who finished first and second, but the 1920 Open, the first after the Great War, produced the best comeback by a champion over the final 36 holes. George Duncan, thirteen strokes behind Abe Mitchell at halfway, won by two strokes from Sandy Herd with Mitchell fourth. Since 1920, there has been no higher winning score, with Duncan the last champion failing to break 80 in all four rounds.

Deal poses a relentless challenge that has remained fresh; its open, somewhat bleak, landscape having changed little since Roger Wethered, who tied for The Open two years earlier, became Amateur champion there in 1923. Today's equipment may have eased the problems somewhat but it still fits Darwin's description of being "fine, straight-ahead, long-hitting golf, wherein the fives are likely to be many and the fours few." Through the eyes of leading amateurs and the club golfer, it is as formidable as ever.

1924 *opposite*

George Duncan, the winner of the 1920 Open Championship, stands in front of the clubhouse during the 1924 Open. Duncan was thirteen strokes behind the leader, Abe Mitchell, after 36 holes but went on to win by two shots.

previous pages

A view toward the clubhouse from beside the green on the 18th hole.

1920

On the 3rd green is Abe Mitchell, who led the Championship by six strokes after 36 holes, but finished tied for fourth place. Opposite is the 3rd green today.

ROYAL LIVERPOOL

Royal Liverpool

Course length 2006 Open
7,258 yards, par 72

1897 / 1902 / 1907 / 1913
1924 / 1930 / 1936 / 1947
1956 / 1967 / 2006

Royal Liverpool has always been a club associated with a series of firsts. Many surround its contribution to the amateur game but, in the context of The Open Championship, it was the first (and only) club to boast one of its members, Harold Hilton, as champion over his home course. It produced the first winner with the then-revolutionary new rubber-cored golf ball (Sandy Herd, 1902), the first winner from overseas (Arnaud Massy from France in 1907), the first Irish winner (Fred Daly, 1947), and the first and only winner from South America (Roberto de Vicenzo, 1967). It also proved to be one of the stepping stones on the path of Bobby Jones to the Grand Slam (1930) and the third of Peter Thomson's successive victories (1956)—the only man to achieve the feat in the twentieth century.

Demands to stage championships long ago were much less onerous than they later became and, in company with Royal St George's and Carnoustie, Hoylake spent thirty-nine years in the wilderness. In the end, its reawakening lay in the acquisition of land for hospitality tents and the transfer of practice facilities to Hoylake Municipal on the other side of the railway, but their return to the fold in 2006 was a glorious success in a week when parched fairways conjured up links golf at its absolute best. Tiger Woods, relishing the challenge, again stole the show.

His recipe was to play short of the bunkers from the tee and rely on superlative iron play in attacking the flags. A revision of the numbering on a course with three new greens entailed the normal 16th becoming the 18th, a hole, when the 16th, that revived memories of the 3-wood shot that enabled Roberto de Vicenzo to realise a dream in 1967. He had previously finished close on several occasions including third place in Thomson's Open eleven years earlier.

Emotional scenes greeted a popular figure but Hoylake and a slice of romance have gone hand in hand since Harold Hilton won its first Open. Hilton also won Muirfield's first Open in 1892 when another famous Hoylake son, John Ball, was equal second. Ball, who played in his first Open in 1878 and his last in 1927, was champion in 1890. It is a legacy no other club can match.

1924 *opposite*

Walter Hagen is congratulated by his wife, Edna, after winning The Open for the second time.

previous pages

The green on the 16th hole, which played as the 18th during the 2006 Open Championship.

1902 *left*

Barefoot children follow the action.

1924 *middle*

Five-time Open winner J. H. Taylor poses for the camera while spectators look on. He was in second place after two rounds and finished fifth.

1947 *below*

A young boy waits behind a crowd gathered around the information board.

1936 *opposite*

The winner, Alf Padgham, surrounded by well-wishers.

Gene Sarazen drives from the 1st tee. The winner of the US Open in 1922 and the US PGA Championship in 1922 and 1923, Sarazen had failed to qualify in the 1923 Open and then finished tied for forty-first place in 1924.

1930 *above*

Bobby Jones makes his speech after winning
The Open for the third time. The previous
month he had helped the US team to victory
at Royal St George's in the Walker Cup, before
going on to win the Amateur Championship
at St Andrews. Following his Open victory,
Jones returned to the States, where he secured
his status as a golfing legend by winning the US
Open and US Amateur Championships, thus
completing the Grand Slam.

following pages

The green on the 11th hole, which was the
13th during the 2006 Championship.

1947

Fred Daly is hoisted off the ground by fans after becoming the first Irishman to win The Open Championship.

1947

A large number of spectators follow
Henry Cotton over the course.

1956

Peter Thomson attracts a large crowd as he plays out of a bunker. He went on to win for the third consecutive year, becoming the first player to achieve a hat-trick over 72 holes of play.

1956
Henry Cotton looks relaxed as he changes his shoes, perched on his car.

2006 *following pages*
Tiger Woods and his caddie, Steve Williams, make their way over the sun-scorched course to the 2nd green during the final round of the Championship.

1967

A large gallery watches at the 12th hole.

1967

All eyes are on the ball, which rolls toward the hole on the 72nd and secures victory for Roberto de Vicenzo.

2006 *following pages*

Richard Sterne plays out of the fairway bunker on the 16th during the first round.

2006

Tiger Woods tees off at the 7th during the final round, and the emotion pours out as he wins his third Open Championship title.

ROYAL BIRKDALE

Royal Birkdale

Course length 2008 Open
7,173 yards, par 70

1954 / 1961 / 1965 / 1971 / 1976
1983 / 1991 / 1998 / 2008

Royal Birkdale, nominated for the 1940 Open, was a late recruit to the fold but it established itself with great haste as a worthy battleground. As one of the more modern links, not least in having two loops of nine holes and less undulating fairways between dunes than most, it combines undoubted playing merit with the space to accommodate all the trappings that are increasingly associated with important events.

Certainly, nobody could fault the quality of its champions—a lineage that includes Peter Thomson (twice), Arnold Palmer, Lee Trevino, Johnny Miller, and Tom Watson. Thomson made history as the first Australian champion in 1954, although his second Birkdale victory was, by common consent, the finest of his five. It was the last championship when the final two rounds were completed on a Friday.

Palmer's second round 73 in 1961 was one of the best bad-weather rounds, but the loss of Friday's play when 36 holes were due to be played meant that, for the second year in succession, the championship ended on a Saturday. However, of major concern was the R&A's declaration that, in the event of Saturday's play being lost as well (Sunday play was out of the question), the championship would be void. Happily, it wasn't.

1971 and 1976 saw the brilliant best of Trevino and Miller, Miller chased home by Nicklaus and a handsome young Spaniard, Seve Ballesteros. If nothing else, the fifth victory of Watson is remembered for his superlative drive and 2-iron on the 72nd hole and in 1991 for the outward half of 29 by Ian Baker-Finch in his final round. He was the fourth Australian champion but, following the deserved success of Mark O'Meara in 1998, Padraig Harrington's sterling finish in 2008 suddenly put clear water between him and his pursuers in a week of wind and rain. The Irishman's victory broke the pattern in that hitherto, Birkdale's champions had been either Australian or American.

2008 *opposite*

Greg Norman congratulates Padraig Harrington on winning The Open after their dramatic head-to-head clash in the final round.

previous pages

The green on the 18th hole, with the last rays of the sun shining on the clubhouse.

1961

'Arnie's Army' looks on as their hero, Arnold Palmer, plays from the rough. He went on to win and then successfully defended his title the following year.

2008 *opposite above*

Spectators follow the progress of Chris Wood during the final round. As leading amateur, he won the Silver Medal.

2008 *opposite below*

Greg Norman plays from the rough on the 8th hole, watched by a large crowd.

1971 *above*

Some fans seek a more advantageous, but precarious, viewing position.

1965 *right*

All eyes are on Tony Lema as he plays from an awkward lie.

1971

The moment of triumph: a victorious Lee
Trevino throws his cap in the air in delight
at winning the Championship.

1971 *above right and right*

Trevino hugs the runner up Mr. Lu and raises the Claret Jug to his lips in celebration.

following pages

View of the 11th green at Birkdale.

1976
Seve Ballesteros plays from a sandhill.

1983 *following pages*
Arnold Palmer *(left)* and Tom Watson
(right) in action. Watson was on his way to
winning his fifth Open title.

1991 *opposite and above*

Ian Baker-Finch on the 18th green, with the Claret Jug almost in his grasp, and then raising his arms in victory after winning by two strokes from Mike Harwood. A spectacular third round of 64 brought Baker-Finch into serious contention and he went into the final round heading the field with Mark O'Meara, who finished tied for third.

1998 *following pages*

The crowds and media surround the 18th green as the winner, Mark O'Meara, holds the Claret Jug.

175

2008 *above*

Camilo Villegas causes a sandstorm as he blasts out of a bunker on the 18th during the third round.

1998 *opposite above*

Justin Rose shows his delight after holing his third shot on the 18th during the final round. He finished tied for fourth place and won the Silver Medal as the leading amateur.

2008 *opposite below*

An emphatic reaction from Ian Poulter as he makes a birdie putt on the 16th during the final round. He finished in second place.

2008 *following pages*

Padraig Harrington plays up to the 18th green and toward victory.

ROYAL LYTHAM
& ST ANNES

1926

Bobby Jones is presented with the Claret Jug, after winning the first of his three Open Championship titles.

1974 *following pages*

Gary Player lines up a putt, watched by a heaving gallery on the grandstand behind.

1952 *above*

The newsreel cameramen stand on their
cars to get a better view.

1963 *above right*

Phil Rodgers hands in his scorecard. By closing a two-stroke deficit in the final round, he forced a 36-hole play-off with Bob Charles. Rodgers lost the play-off the next day.

1963 *right*

Jack Nicklaus gives an informal press conference outside the Recorder's caravan.

1952 & 1958

opposite and this page

Giants of their era: Bobby Locke *(left)* and Peter Thomson *(right)* dominated The Open from 1949 right through the 1950s. Locke won four times (1949, 1950, 1952, 1957) and Thomson won five (1954, 1955, 1956, 1958, 1965). The seven-year gap which separated Thomson's fourth and fifth victories saw the big three—Palmer, Player, and Nicklaus—rise to prominence.

following pages

An impending storm looms over the green on the 6th hole.

1979 *opposite and below*

Seve Ballesteros after winning the first of his
three Open Championship titles.

1988 *following pages*

A crowd of spectators surrounds Seve
Ballesteros during the first round of the
Championship, which he went on to win.
It was his third Open victory and his
second win at Lytham.

1996

Tom Lehman acknowledges the crowd after winning with a score of 271. Ernie Els and Mark McCumber finished two strokes behind.

2001 *following pages*

David Duval plays from the rough on the final day of the Championship. An exceptional round of 65 on day three pulled him from joint thirty-fifth position to joint leader and a controlled final round score of 67 saw him finish three shots clear of the runner-up, Niclas Fasth.

ROYAL PORTRUSH

Royal Portrush

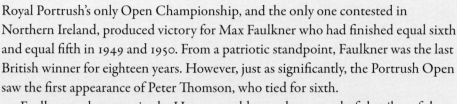

Course length 1951 Open
6,802 yards

1951

Royal Portrush's only Open Championship, and the only one contested in Northern Ireland, produced victory for Max Faulkner who had finished equal sixth and equal fifth in 1949 and 1950. From a patriotic standpoint, Faulkner was the last British winner for eighteen years. However, just as significantly, the Portrush Open saw the first appearance of Peter Thomson, who tied for sixth.

Faulkner, a showman in the Hagen mould, was also a wonderful striker of the ball. His success, like that of many champions, owed much to the good fortune of completing his second round of 70 before an afternoon of wind and rain plagued his challengers. It also owed much to the fact that, of his 285 shots, only 108 were putts. Admirers of Portrush, the birthplace of the 1947 champion Fred Daly, regretted that it only had one year of Open prominence.

It has no let-ups, as the names of some of the holes suggest. Himalayas, Calamity, and Purgatory strike a note of terror but Tavern and Feather Bed indicate a lighter side. Harry Colt's, the 6th, commemorates the golf course architect whom Bernard Darwin wrote had "built himself a monument more enduring than brass", and Portrush's coastal glory is recognised in Causeway and Skerries. It is a superb links on a grand scale that still tests the best.

1951 *opposite*

Max Faulkner smiles broadly as he receives the Claret Jug.

previous pages

View of the 14th hole, known as 'Calamity.'

following pages

The green on the 6th hole, with the 6th hole on the Valley Course behind.

1951

Spectators congregate in front of the scoreboard.

1951

Bobby Locke, on the far right, plays from
the light rough to the 9th hole.

TURNBERRY

Turnberry

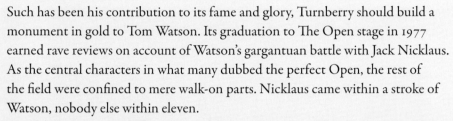

Course length 2009 Open
7204 yards, par 70

1977 / 1986 / 1994 / 2009

Such has been his contribution to its fame and glory, Turnberry should build a monument in gold to Tom Watson. Its graduation to The Open stage in 1977 earned rave reviews on account of Watson's gargantuan battle with Jack Nicklaus. As the central characters in what many dubbed the perfect Open, the rest of the field were confined to mere walk-on parts. Nicklaus came within a stroke of Watson, nobody else within eleven.

Although it was a difficult act to follow, the next two Turnberry Opens were highly significant in the crowning of Greg Norman in 1986 and Nick Price in 1994 but, in 2009, it was Watson again who performed an impossible encore. Thirty-four years after his first appearance at Carnoustie, he led with one round to play and then with one hole to play. Within forty-six days of his sixtieth birthday, his chivalrous spirit and enduring skill stood on the brink of The Open's, maybe the whole of sports', most astonishing achievement.

Casting aspersions at the golfing fates is an unworthy pursuit but uncommitted onlookers, if there were any, would swear Watson's fine second shot at the 72nd hole was treated unkindly as it trickled down the bank at the back of the green and the task of getting up and down was just beyond him. An immediate play-off was an even crueler twist for tiring limbs but the golfing world was still lost in admiration and Watson was as gracious in defeat as ever he was in victory. Stewart Cink, recognising his chance, was the grateful and worthy beneficiary.

Without earlier, happy memories of Turnberry, it is doubtful if an alternative links would have been the same source of inspiration for Watson. There is nowhere that possesses such magical powers when the sun sparkles but, in 1986, Norman had to withstand two stormy days in between a second round of 63 that included three putts on the 18th green and a final 69 that took him home by five strokes.

Eight years later, Price's stirring finish gave him a single stroke to spare, but it was an Open that everyone wanted him to win. At the prize giving, he remarked, "In 1982, I had my left hand on the trophy and in 1988 I had my right hand on the trophy. Now, I've finally got both hands on the trophy and, boy, does it feel good."

1977 *opposite*

The 'Duel in the Sun' is over and Tom Watson is the winner. He and Jack Nicklaus walk off the 18th green together after one of the most dramatic and memorable Open Championships in history.

previous pages
The rugged Turnberry coastline bordering the links.

1977 *above*

Watson and Nicklaus in action during the
final round.

1977 *middle*

Watson and Nicklaus take time out to
shelter on the rocks when a thunderstorm
strikes during the third round.

1977 *above*

Watson celebrates after his birdie putt at the 72nd hole brought the duel to an end. He won in 268, a new record score for The Open, which would stand until 1993. He shattered the previous record of 276, set by Arnold Palmer in 1962, and tied by Tom Weiskopf in 1973.

1986 *following pages*

Greg Norman drives from the 9th tee in his final round.

2009 *previous pages*

A picturesque view from behind the green
on the remodelled 16th hole.

1986 *opposite*

Greg Norman hits his approach shot to the
18th green during the second round, which
saw him produce a new course record of 63.

1986 *above*

Norman celebrates with his caddie after
winning his first Open Championship title
by a comfortable margin of five strokes.

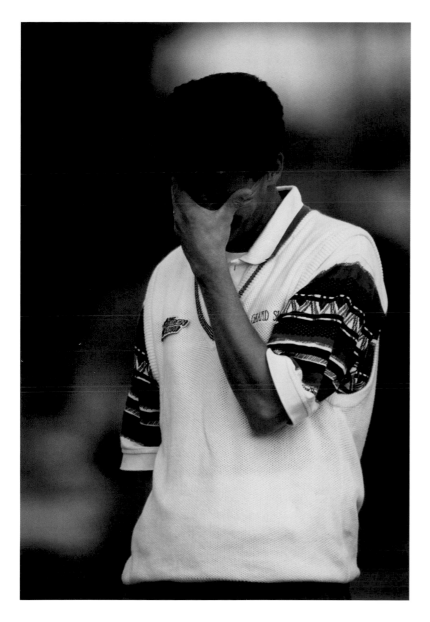

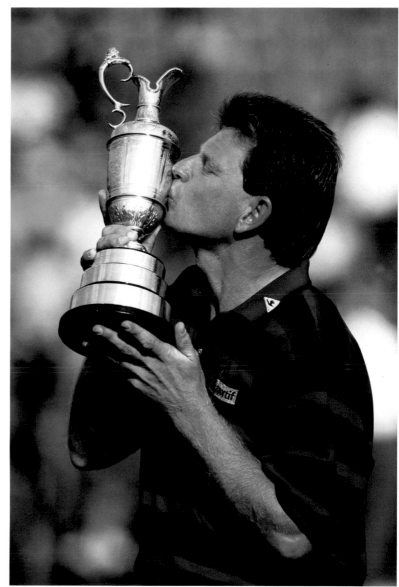

1994 *opposite above and below*

Jesper Parnevik in trouble at the 15th during the 4th round, where he would drop a shot. Meanwhile, Nick Price leaps in the air after sinking an eagle putt at the 17th.

1994 *above left and right*

Despair for Parnevik, whose bogey five at the 72nd cost him dearly, and joy for Nick Price as he finally lays both hands on the Claret Jug.

2009 *above left*

Youth and wisdom meet: Tom Watson
and Matteo Manassero on the 16th green
during the second round, after Watson
holes a birdie putt.

2009 *left*

Sergio Garcia shows his respect for Tom
Watson by applauding as he walks up the
18th fairway on the second day.

2009 *above*

Stewart Cink celebrates as he holes a birdie putt on the 18th during the final round.

2009

Watson looks on as his ball edges
devastatingly close to the hole—but he
knows he has missed, and a play-off will
follow.

2009 *above right*

Watson maintains his composure as Cink shows his emotions after winning the playoff.

right

Watson looks on as Cink studies the Claret Jug.

following pages

Watson gazes out to sea from the Turnberry coastline during the final round.

PRESTWICK

Prestwick

Course length 1925 Open
6,444 yards

1860 / 1861 / 1862 / 1863 / 1864 / 1865
1866 / 1867 / 1868 / 1869 / 1870 / 1872
1875 / 1878 / 1881 / 1884 / 1887 / 1890
1893 / 1898 / 1903 / 1908 / 1914 / 1925

To Prestwick belongs the momentous claim of being the cradle of championship golf. The club launched The Open and staged it on twenty-four occasions. What is more, the first course consisted intriguingly of 12 holes, whose criss-cross design must have made playing and watching decidedly precarious.

For historical correctness, the first Open took place on Wednesday 17 October 1860. It was contested by eight players, decided over three rounds of the 12-hole course, and won by Willie Park, Sr. with two strokes to spare over Tom Morris, Sr, a St Andrean who was appointed custodian of the Prestwick links at the Club's formation in 1851. The whole credit for The Open's development belongs to the Prestwick Club, which saw the championship as bringing to an end what Robert Browning in *The History of Golf* called "the golden age of private matches."

Its subsequent banishment to The Open sidelines proved that, in many ways, it was a victim of its own success. The crowds it attracted were so large that it was felt it couldn't handle them in the new era of admission tickets that dawned in 1926, although the course became 18 holes in time for the 1884 Open. However, in common with Deal, Prince's, and Portrush, there was never any suggestion of a waning in the challenge of the links. In many ways, it is a better modern test than in the days of hickories. It comprises many outstanding individual holes that examine a wide range of shot-making while some of the heavily contoured greens are more appropriately approached with a fuller armoury of pitching clubs. It is certainly just as much fun.

Jim Barnes, a naturalised American born in Cornwall, was Prestwick's final Open champion but, for historical purposes, the deeds of Young Tom Morris and Harry Vardon are those principally remembered. Tommy's feat of playing 12 holes in 47 strokes in 1870, including a 3 at the 578-yard 1st hole, set new standards of scoring. He, more than anyone, shaped Prestwick's fame, but the other legendary figure with proud associations was Vardon. After a rota of courses was introduced in 1872, he is the only player to have won The Open three times on the same course, including in 1903, when his own brother, Tom, finished second.

1925 *opposite*

Macdonald Smith drives from the 13th tee during the last Open Championship to be played at Prestwick.

previous pages

The green on the 17th hole, 'The Alps.'

J. H. Taylor drives from the 1st tee. He finished tied for ninth place.

middle

Harry Vardon crosses the Player's Bridge at 'The Himalayas' during the final round.

below

Harry Vardon putts on the 18th to win the fourth of his six Open titles. He won with a score of 300, six strokes clear of his brother, Tom. Vardon won three of six Open titles at Prestwick.

1908 opposite

James Braid, Open Champion for the fourth time, stands outside the clubhouse with his caddie and a group of spectators. Braid shot 291 to finish eight strokes ahead of Tom Ball.

following pages

View of the 18th green and clubhouse.

1925 *opposite*

Panoramic view of the course and spectators watching play.

1925 *above*

Macdonald Smith (right) crosses the Burn, while a crowd prepares to follow.

following pages

The light from the setting sun just touches the fairway on the 14th hole.

ROYAL TROON

Royal Troon

Troon assumed the role of Prestwick as Ayrshire's Open Championship standard-bearer although there were twenty-seven years between its first and second championships. Like Lytham, it is a course designed on the out and back principle with the outward nine containing the shortest (8th), 123 yards, hole in championship golf. Until 2005, it also had the longest (6th), 601 yards.

In a world obsessed with length, the Postage Stamp is a monument to shrewd cunning, a hole in 1989 where the mighty Greg Norman dropped his only stroke in a final round of 64. You have to whisper that Tiger Woods notched up a 6 there in 1997 as well.

If the wind is helping on the opening holes along the shore, the turn for home presents a vastly different story but, in 1962, the roles were reversed. It was the outward nine that gave Arnold Palmer more headaches in a week of fast running fairways. On the par 5, 4th, out of range for almost everyone except Palmer, he had two 6's and two 5's but his dashing play on the longer back nine certainly laid the foundation for his glittering success.

The newly lengthened 11th alongside the railway was the key but, in four rounds, Palmer tamed it in typically cavalier fashion, eventually winning by six strokes from Kel Nagle with 276, the lowest aggregate at the time. It was also the year that saw the start of Jack Nicklaus's distinguished participation as well as the need for a tougher approach to crowd control.

Troon's sole home winner was Arthur Havers in 1923, although Bobby Locke was a familiar figure in Britain at the time of his triumph in 1950. After Palmer, American dominance continued with the elegant power of Tom Weiskopf, who led throughout in 1973, and the success of Tom Watson in 1982, a championship that one or two others could, and perhaps should, have won.

There then followed Mark Calcavecchia's survival of The Open's first three-way play-off and the first over four holes, the triumph of Justin Leonard, and Todd Hamilton's defeat of Ernie Els in a play-off. Els, therefore, joined the elite company of those who have won and lost an Open title in a play-off.

A sentimental footnote was the hole-in-one in 1973 of Gene Sarazen at the 8th with a 5-iron, fifty years after his first appearance—when he failed to qualify.

Course length 2004 Open
7,175 yards, par 71

1923 / 1950 / 1962 / 1973 / 1982
1989 / 1997 / 2004

2004 *opposite*

Ian Poulter in action at the 6th hole during the second round. He finished tied for twenty-fifth place.

previous pages

Panoramic view of the 8th hole, known as the 'Postage Stamp.'

1923 *opposite above*

Ted Ray hits from the rough. Ray, who
won The Open in 1912 and the US Open
in 1920, finished tied for twelfth place.

1923 *opposite below*

Arthur Havers comes out of a bunker.
He went on to win The Open, finishing
one stroke ahead of Walter Hagen.

1989 *above*

Greg Norman's bid for the title ends when
his drive lands in this bunker at the last
hole of the 4-hole play-off. A stunning
final round of 64 allowed Norman to make
up seven shots on the leaders and force a
play-off with Mark Calcavecchia and Wayne
Grady. Calcavecchia emerged the champion.

1962
Crowds rush down the fairway to
follow the action.

1962 *right*

Kel Nagle plays from the light rough during the final round.

1962 *below*

The scoreboard shows Palmer at 5 under and Nagle at 2 under. Tied for 3rd place after round one, Palmer then led after the second round, while Nagle followed in his wake. With a record-setting winning aggregate of 276, Palmer finished six shots clear of Nagle.

1962

Spectators line the course, watching Arnold Palmer as he plays his tee shot at the 7th hole.

following pages
The 'Postage Stamp' green.

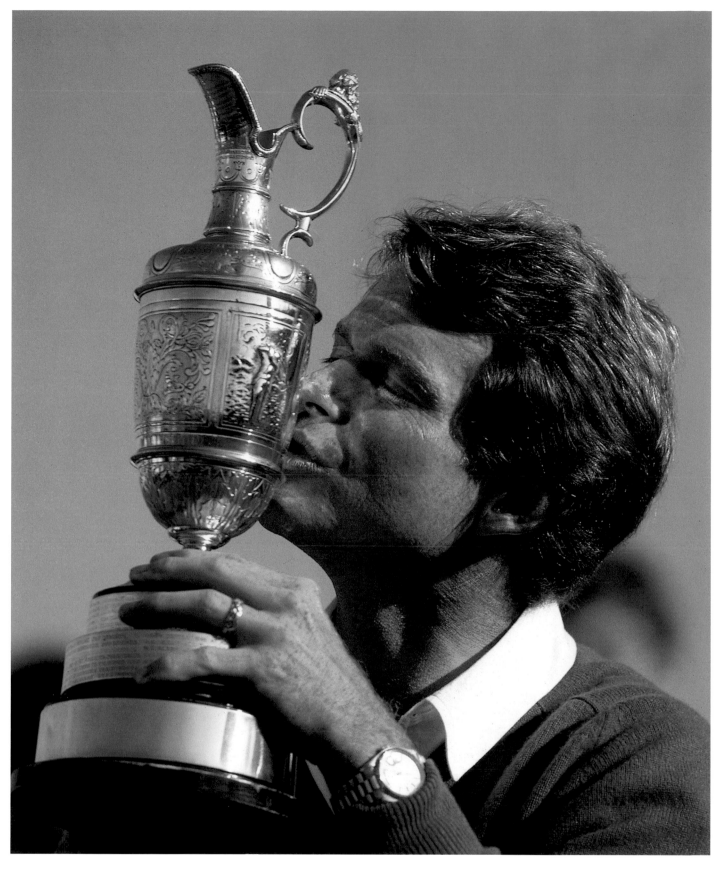

1982 *opposite and above*

Tom Watson in action and, for a fourth time, with the coveted Claret Jug in his possession.

1989 *above*

Mark Calcavecchia celebrates after winning the 4-hole play-off.

1989 *opposite*

A colourful array of umbrellas protect the crowd from the rain at the 13th hole during the second round.

1997 *following pages*

An emotional moment for Justin Leonard as he stands on the 18th green with the Claret Jug.

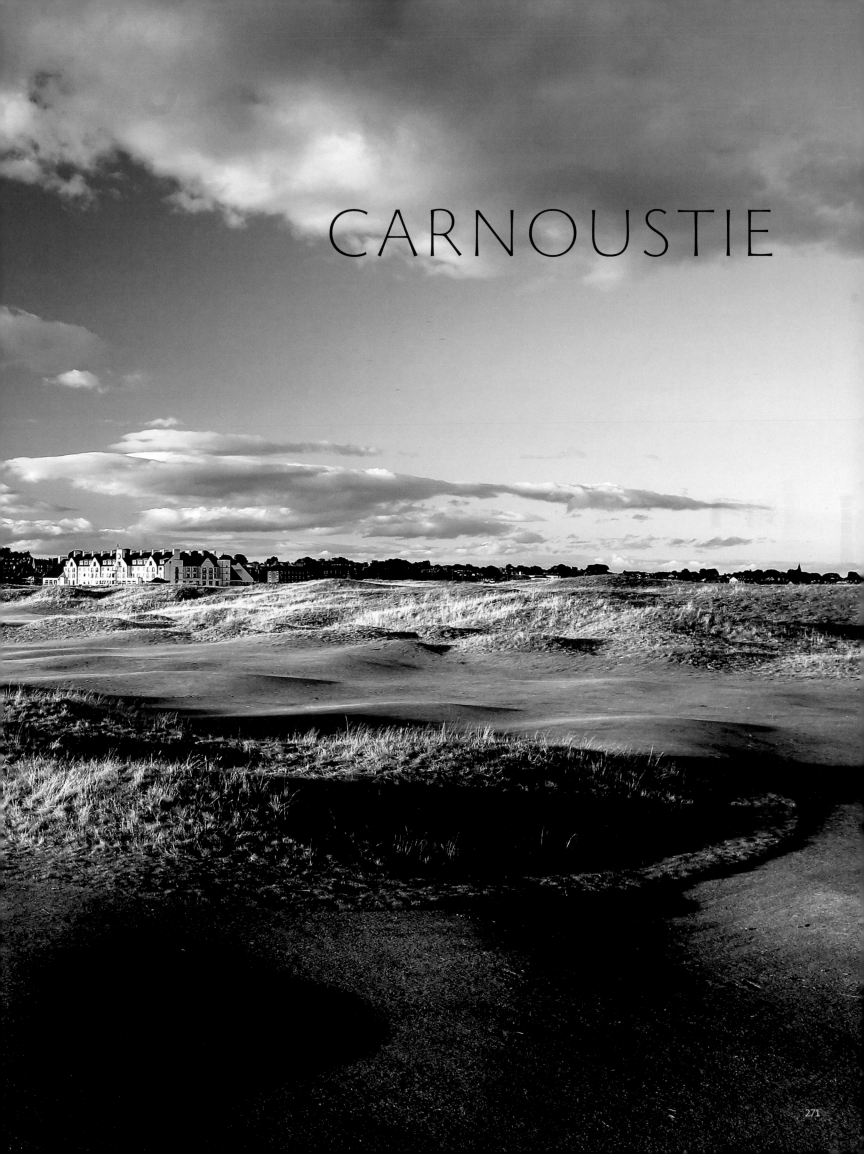

CARNOUSTIE

Carnoustie

Carnoustie, the nursery of so many Scottish golfers, "is long, interesting and difficult, possessing in particular a fine, crucial finish amid the lethal windings of the Barry Burn." Bernard Darwin's summary stops short of saying that Carnoustie is the toughest of all The Open Championship courses—but, by common consent, it is. The two most recent events in 1999 and 2007 were demonstrable proof.

Carnoustie came relatively late on the scene in 1931, with Tommy Armour narrowly prevailing. However, the next three were perfect portrayals of how a stern, honest staging ground was ideal in confirming the supremacy of three legendary figures: Henry Cotton, Ben Hogan, and Gary Player.

In 1937, Cotton defeated the might of the American Ryder Cup team in terrible weather on the final day, but his striking was flawless as he made up three strokes on Reg Whitcombe in the fourth round. Remarkably, it is said that Cotton drove himself a good part of his way home that night—but sixteen years later, Hogan's even longer journey prevented him contesting the USPGA championship, and so lost him the chance to add that title to his Open, Masters, and US Open victories in the same year—a feat nobody has achieved.

Player's triumph in 1968 was undoubtedly his best, but the other three Opens were all decided in play-offs—although Carnoustie was confined to the Open sidelines for twenty-four years after 1975, when Tom Watson joined the elite by winning on his first appearance, one of only four who have done so since 1933.

Jack Newton, his play-off opponent who had a third round of 65, was defiant to the last, but those who like fraught climaxes had their wish in 1999 when Paul Lawrie was crowned champion and, again in 2007, when Padraig Harrington broke the lasting resistance of Sergio Garcia. Lawrie made up ten strokes in the final round, returning an aggregate of 290, the highest since 1947, but was the beneficiary of Jean Van de Velde's celebrated skirmish with the Barry Burn on the 72nd hole when a 6 would have given him victory.

Course length 2007 Open
7,421 yards, par 71

1931 / 1937 / 1953 / 1968 / 1975
1999 / 2007

1953 *opposite*

Ben Hogan takes a break before teeing off.

previous pages

View of the 3rd hole with the Carnoustie
Golf Hotel in the background.

1931 *below*

Tommy Armour is presented with the trophy by the Earl of Airlie. He was the first player to win The Open at Carnoustie.

1937 *left*

Henry Cotton receives the Claret Jug after winning the second of his three Open titles.

1931 *above*

Tommy Armour plays out of trouble.

following pages

Aerial view showing the 16th and 17th holes, with the Barry Burn winding its way through the course.

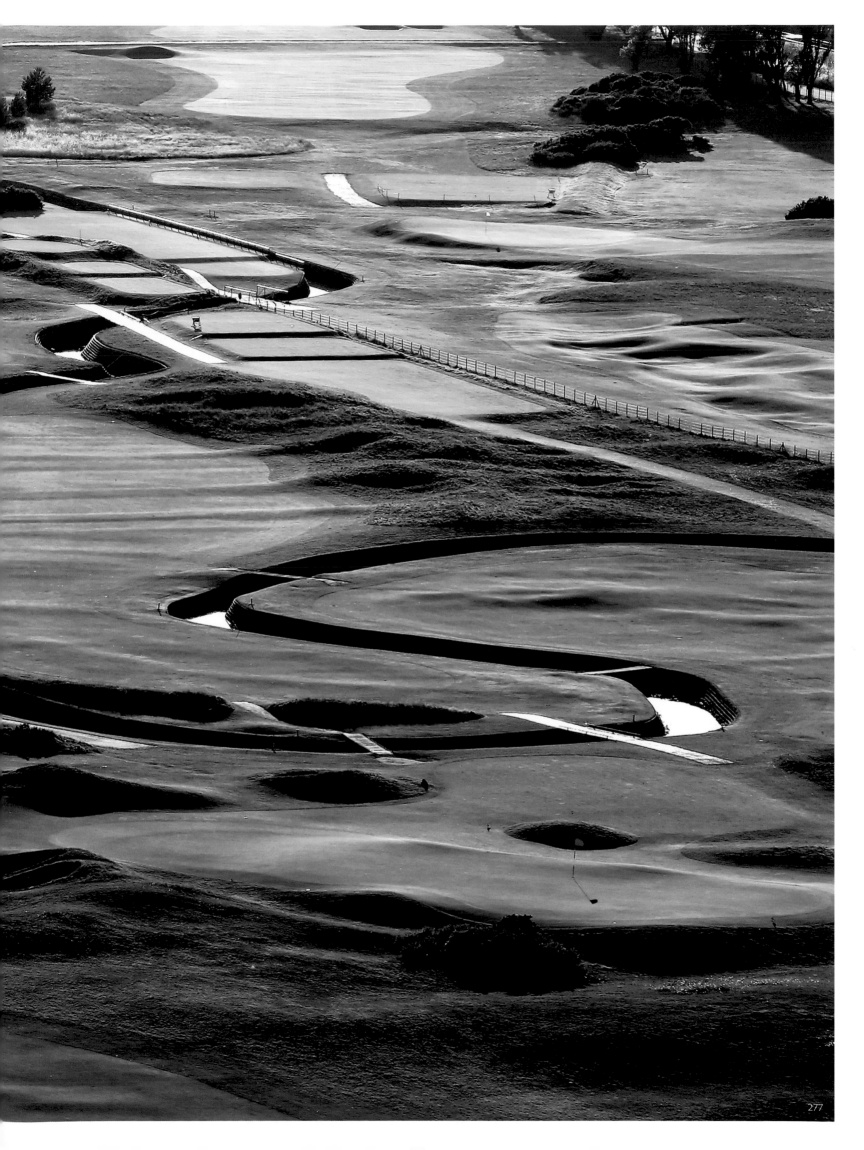

1953 *above*

Ben Hogan drives off, watched by a large
crowd of spectators.

1953 *opposite*

Hogan and Bill Branch leave the 18th
green at the end of their qualifying round.
Hogan went on to win the Claret Jug
while Branch failed to qualify for the
Championship.

1968 *above*

Defending champion Roberto de Vicenzo finds time to relax.

1999 *opposite*

Tiger Woods battles tough conditions at the 4th hole on the final day of the Championship.

1968 *above*

Gary Player plays the 72nd hole on his way
to claiming his second Open title. He won
with an aggregate of 289, two strokes clear of
Jack Nicklaus and Bob Charles.

1975 *opposite above and right*

Jack Newton and Tom Watson both hold
the Claret Jug as they face an 18-hole play-
off. Watson won by a single stroke to secure
his first Open title.

1999

Jean Van de Velde assesses the position of his ball after finding the Barry Burn with his third shot on the 18th hole. A triple bogey seven destroyed his three-stroke lead and he finished on 290, matching the aggregate of Paul Lawrie and Justin Leonard, both of whom believed their challenge to be over. In the resulting 4-hole play-off, Lawrie emerged triumphant.

1999

Paul Lawrie revels in his Championship victory.

2007

K. J. Choi watches his tee shot on the 9th hole during the third round. He finished tied for eighth place.

2007

Harrington celebrates his victory. The Claret Jug returned to Ireland for the first time since 1947, when Fred Daly won the Championship.

2007 *following pages*

Padraig Harrington poses with the Claret Jug after winning his first major championship title.

View of the Old Course, St Andrews, from the balcony
of The R&A Chief Executive's office.

Afterword

On reaching this milestone in Open history we can, I think, look back over the past 150 years with pride; pride at how the Championship has grown and developed. From very small beginnings in 1860 a truly global sporting event has emerged.

As custodian of The Open, The R&A is charged with no light burden of responsibility. It must maintain the Championship's position at the forefront of golf in the years to come.

There are great traditions to be upheld. We will, I am certain, continue to stage The Open on the finest links courses the United Kingdom has to offer, on those firm and fast-playing surfaces we all wish to see. Our qualifying events will provide opportunities for lesser-ranked players from all around the world to secure a place alongside the stars in the starting lineup. The Open will remain truly open and the most international of golf's majors.

While we have a duty to preserve the best traditions of the Championship, we have an equally demanding responsibility to ensure that The Open keeps pace with, or indeed outstrips, best modern practice.

Our courses must continue to challenge the world's best; spectator and player amenities must be second to none; our television and digital media output must attract large worldwide audiences; we must be quick to embrace all relevant new technology, and so on. And because so much of Open revenue is put toward golf development projects, we have a duty to safeguard the profitability of the event. No small task indeed.

We owe a great debt to all who have contributed to making The Open what it is today. Others will carry on the task in the future and to them I say, "Good luck and look after it well. It is something very special."

What would those eight professionals who played in 1860 at Prestwick think of The Open today? They would certainly be astonished, but I hope they would also be pleased; pleased that what they began has grown into such a highlight of the sporting calendar.

PETER DAWSON
Chief Executive, The R&A

The Cartgate Bunker guarding the
3rd green at St Andrews.

Great Open Champions

Without champions, there would be no story. All have their rightful place in a proud dynasty, but some have earned greater eminence than others. Prolific winners are obvious choices but some with fewer victories have left a mark that has contributed significantly in changing the face of the championship and the course of its history.

WILLIE PARK SR
1860, 1863, 1866, 1875

A bold driver and an outstanding putter, Willie Park Sr won the first Open Championship in 1860, finishing two shots clear of his great rival Tom Morris Sr. Park would repeat as champion in 1863, 1866 and 1875. He was also the head of the formidable Park dynasty which lent such distinction to the championship's early history.

Willie's brother, Mungo, triumphed in the first Open at Musselburgh in 1874 and another brother, David, finished second to Willie in 1866. Later, Willie's son, Willie Park Jr, was champion in 1887 and 1889, prior to becoming one of the first eminent golf course architects. Thirteen of the first fifteen Opens were won by a Park or a Morris, a family rivalry that was great, glamorous and glorious.

TOM MORRIS SR
1861, 1862, 1864, 1867

Tom Morris Sr won The Open at the second time of asking in 1861 and went on to win another three times, in 1862, 1864 and 1867, when he was forty-six years old. As a golfer, he was long and straight off the tee and his approach shots to the green were one of his strengths. A good long putter, he was less reliable close to the hole. He was Keeper of the

Green at St Andrews from 1864 until 1903 and became the symbolic face of golf in the late 19th century.

TOMMY MORRIS
1868, 1869, 1870, 1872

Tom Morris Sr's achievements in The Open were surpassed by his son, Tommy. Toppling his father as champion at the age of seventeen in 1868, he won four titles in a row. He had power and dash in his long game and a quality of brilliance that could produce an extraordinarily great shot when it was needed. During the course of his greatest triumph in 1870, Tommy covered three rounds of Prestwick's 12 hole course in 149. It was the first great scoring achievement by the game's first real hero.

THE GREAT TRIUMVIRATE:

HARRY VARDON
1896, 1898, 1899, 1903, 1911, 1914

JAMES BRAID
1901, 1905, 1906, 1908, 1910

J.H. TAYLOR
1894, 1895, 1900, 1909, 1913

No period in the history of the Open was so dominated by three players as that by Harry Vardon [left], James Braid and J.H. Taylor between 1894 and 1914. Together, they won the title sixteen times out of twenty-one. Vardon won a yet unsurpassed six times, while Taylor and Braid both won The Open five times. Born within thirteen months of one another, they forged a rivalry that electrified the golf world but, in terms of playing method, they

provided a notable contrast. Vardon was the first classic stylist. Braid [bottom left] was said to hit "with divine fury" while Taylor's game was made up of solid virtues. World War I curtailed their successes but they left an indelible mark. Since 1873, Vardon is the only player to have won The Open three times over the same course (Prestwick). Braid is the only player to have won twice on two courses (St Andrews and Muirfield) while Taylor [above] had the largest span between first and last victories (nineteen years) as well as sixteen top five finishes, the last aged fifty-three.

WALTER HAGEN
1922, 1924, 1928, 1929

Walter Hagen was the game's first showman, a godsend to headline writers. He helped make golf front page news. His flamboyance and example earned professional golfers new respect, recognition and prosperity. The first American-born winner of The Open, he had four victories, his last with a score of 292 in 1929 by a margin of six strokes. It included a second round of 67, the lowest in The Open at that time.

His reputation for high living contrasted with an austere upbringing in which he earned ten cents an hour as a caddie, but his rise as a player was swift. Having finished joint fourth to Francis Ouimet in the famous US Open in 1913, he was champion himself the following year at the age of twenty-one and won again in 1919 before becoming one of the first Americans to travel to The Open on a regular basis. Between 1921 and 1929, Hagen had a finishing sequence of equal 6th, 1st, 2nd, 1st, equal 3rd and 1st. He didn't play in 1925 and 1927.

BOBBY JONES
1926, 1927, 1930

Bobby Jones played in four Opens and won three. In his first at St Andrews in 1921, he tore up his card in the third round, a wholly uncharacteristic failing, but his overall contributions to the championship were immeasurable. He was the last amateur winner and the first to capture The Open and US Open in the same year (1926), all with hickory-shafted clubs. At St Andrews in 1927, he played quite brilliantly but, in 1926 and 1930, he showed how to win without playing his best.

Curiously, he found victory in The Amateur Championship harder than in The Open but, in 1930, he succeeded at St Andrews and so set in motion a sequence of events which history will never see repeated. He captured The Open at Hoylake before returning home to add the US Open and US Amateur—all in the same year.

Borrowing a bridge expression, it was an achievement acclaimed as the Grand Slam although many prefer the Impregnable Quadrilateral. With no more worlds to conquer, he retired from competitive golf at the age of twenty-eight.

SIR HENRY COTTON
1934, 1937, 1948

Cotton's three victories were all notable. In 1934, in ending an eleven-year drought without a home winner, he set scoring records that defied belief. In 1937, he defeated the might of the American Ryder Cup team and, in 1948, as something of a lap of honour, won by five strokes at Muirfield watched by King George VI. All three could have been said to have been his finest hour.

In common with many champions, Cotton used the championship at Royal St George's to generate a resurgence of form but even he must have surprised himself with his first two rounds of 67 and 65 which followed a 66 in the first qualifying round that he considered the best of all. It was twenty-four years before his 65 was equalled in an Open and

forty-three before it was bettered. Cotton's brilliance in 1934 enabled him to lead by nine strokes after two rounds and by ten strokes after three but, even with an anxious final round of 79, he still won by five. It remains the highest final round by a champion since Vardon's in 1911. When Henry Longhurst was asked the best striker of a ball he ever saw, "I replied unerringly and unhesitatingly, Henry Cotton."

BOBBY LOCKE
1949, 1950, 1952, 1957

Locke was the Open champion four times within the space of nine years and equal second in 1946 and 1954. He is also one of only seven players since World War II to have defended a title successfully. Curiously, he opened with a 69 in all his victorious years but Locke was a patient, thoughtful golfer who played the percentages in shrewd fashion and was the best putter of his generation. He did everything at a measured pace after feeling he lost the 1946 Open through playing too quickly.

His victory in the 1957 Open, transferred from Muirfield to St Andrews on account of the petrol shortage, had a hair-raising conclusion when, having hit his second to within two feet on the 72nd green, he replaced his ball incorrectly after marking it and holed for a three. The Committee felt that, as he had three for the championship and his error had gained him nothing, the "decision should be given in the spirit of the game" and there should be no penalty.

BEN HOGAN
1953

He came. He saw. He conquered. He didn't defend. He never came back. Hogan is the only player to have conducted a special mission to The Open with the express intention of crowning a celebrated career by capturing the one major title that had eluded him. He took some persuading, although, once convinced, his preparation at Carnoustie was probably more thorough than any before and certainly since; and each of his rounds lower than the one before —73,71,70 and 68.

Carnoustie was his first experience of golf in Britain and his first experience of the small ball but a measure of his superb striking on an immensely long course can be seen from the fact that, of his total of 282, 130 were putts. In terms of the crowds he attracted, 1953 was a landmark but he was surprised so many wanted him to win. In 1968, the winning aggregate at Carnoustie was seven strokes more than Hogan's and, in 1999, eight more but Hogan is the only contestant who can claim, played one, won one.

PETER THOMSON
1954, 1955, 1956, 1958, 1965

Thomson is the only player to have won The Open three years in a row since it became a 72 hole championship in 1892. He is also the champion who came nearest to making it five in succession. In defence of his title in 1957, he finished second to Bobby Locke at St Andrews before winning again in 1958. His fifth victory in 1965, the last to be decided by 36-holes on a Friday, was generally regarded as his best in that he was confronted by Palmer, Nicklaus and Lema. Lema was the defending champion, Nicklaus would win the following year, and Palmer was the previous champion at Birkdale. Nobody relished fast links courses more than Thomson or was more accomplished at subduing them. An instinctive ability to flight the ball low was the natural by-product of an engagingly simple, orthodox, rhythmical and reliable swing.

Having made his first Open appearance at Royal Portrush in 1951, Thomson wasn't outside the top six again until 1959, his sequence from 1952 of 2nd, equal 2nd, 1st, 1st, 1st, 2nd and 1st being unmatched. He was the first Australian winner.

GARY PLAYER
1959, 1968, 1974

One of only three to have been champion in three different decades, Player's first triumph at Muirfield in 1959 came after finishing with a six at the par 4, 18th in the final round. This subjected him to an agonising wait to see if he had won. He was eight strokes behind the leader at the half-way stage but his 70, 68 for the final 36 holes illustrated the never-say-die approach that characterised his golf for more than twenty-five years.

His 75 was the highest opening round by a champion since 1929 but he is one of only five champions to have played each round in a lower score than the one before. By contrast to Muirfield, he was never behind in 1974 at Lytham, the first championship to be played with the big ball, but many regarded his second victory at Carnoustie as his finest in view of those who chased him home although his winning total of 289 was the highest for twenty-one years.

ARNOLD PALMER
1961, 1962

Whether he was initiator or beneficiary of the rich era that professional golf entered in the 1960s, Palmer's influence launched a revival of The Open's well-being that was spectacular, influential and long-lasting.

Appearing for the first time in the Centenary Open at St Andrews in 1960, and finishing second, one stroke behind Kel Nagle, he won the next two in contrasting conditions. Birkdale was dogged with bad weather that caused a day's delay but the following year he left the field trailing by six strokes on fast-running fairways at Troon.

His display at Troon was a classic illustration of leading by example, the perfect riposte for losing the US Open in a play-off to Jack Nicklaus at Oakmont only a month before. In his first appearance in The Open, Nicklaus made the cut on the dividing line, but Palmer's mastery was absolute. Whether it was his control in wind and rain at Birkdale or his calculated aggression over Troon's hard ground, his back-to-back victories gave the old championship the impetus it needed.

JACK NICKLAUS
1966, 1970, 1978

Nobody since the Great Triumvirate was in contention in more Opens over a longer period than Jack Nicklaus. In addition to his three titles, he finished runner-up on seven occasions and was third three times. Like Tiger Woods some years later, he was always the man to beat. His first victory was at Muirfield and the other two at St Andrews. In 1970, he needed a play-off to shake off Doug Sanders who finished joint second to Nicklaus in 1966 but in 1978 a stout finish was necessary when several others had chances.

Nicklaus's first taste of Muirfield came as an impressionable teenage Walker Cup player in 1959 although his first success in The Open seven years later was achieved largely by leaving his driver in the bag. This was proof of his mastery of course management that permeated his career in which he had more last day appearances in The Open (thirty-two) than anyone.

TONY JACKLIN
1969

History sets Tony Jacklin apart as the only British golfer to have held The Open and US Open titles at the same time, albeit only for a month. In the late 1960s and early 1970s, British golf needed a hero to compete successfully at international level. Jacklin was ideally cast. He was the torch bearer for the European challenge that quickly took shape but, considering the pressures he confronted, and the national hopes he carried at Lytham in 1969, few champions have matched his composure, assurance and rhythm in the final round.

His drive and 7-iron on the final hole provided the perfect ending that champions seek but, within twelve months, Jacklin had captured the US Open by a staggering seven strokes—a year when Palmer, Player and Nicklaus has opening rounds of 79, 80 and 81. Less than a month later, in defence of his title, Jacklin set St Andrews alight, reaching the turn on the first afternoon in 29 and starting home with a birdie. However, his round was interrupted by a storm when playing the 14th and his momentum was lost.

In 1971 and 1972, he finished third, two strokes behind Lee Trevino, completing four consecutive years when he contested the outcome to the end. He was decidedly unlucky not to have added a second title but he put British golf back on the map.

LEE TREVINO
1971, 1972

Lee Trevino was just what the game needed—a refreshing character from a humble background, a gifted shot maker who was a serious threat to the supremacy of Jack Nicklaus.

His consistency in winning The Open and the US Open twice each in five years placed him in exalted company. In 1971, in fact, he won the US, Canadian and British Opens within the space of twenty-three days, clear evidence of his mental and technical resilience. At Royal Birkdale in 1971, his competitive momentum enabled him to reach the turn in 31 on the final afternoon and establish a commanding position but a 7 on the 17th necessitated finishing with a stout four at the last to hold off the engaging Mr. Lu.

A fourth-round 77 spoiled Trevino's chances at St Andrews in 1970 but his title defence at Muirfield in 1972 owed everything to an inspired short game and a spell of good fortune. Over the last 21 holes, he holed an outrageous bunker shot and two chips, the final one on the 71st for a 5 acting as a dagger through the heart of his playing partner, Tony Jacklin.

TOM WATSON
1975, 1977, 1980, 1982, 1983

In 1983, Jack Nicklaus had made twenty-two appearances in The Open and won three times. Tom Watson had played nine times and won five. That didn't make Watson better than Nicklaus—nobody was—but Watson's five victories, all on different courses, four of them in Scotland, showed an enchanted, unmatched spell of dominance. However, as events proved, that was merely the end of the beginning. Watson almost confounded The Open's historians by winning as Old Tom as well as Young Tom.

In his quest to match Harry Vardon's six successes, he had chances in 1984, 1989 and 1994 but thirty-four years after his first Open, which he won, he turned back the clock in remarkable fashion by needing a four on Turnberry's 72nd hole to win and so topple Tom Morris Sr. as the oldest winner, a record set in 1867. Morris was forty-six years old, Watson fast approaching sixty. He is, by some way, the oldest runner-up on Open record. Turnberry in 2009 showed how the enduring nature of the brisk, even tempo of his swing, crisp striking and command of flight have earned him a special niche in Open history.

SEVE BALLESTEROS
1979, 1984, 1988

After failing to make the final 36 holes the previous year, Ballesteros made a spectacular impact in 1976, aged nineteen, finishing joint second to Johnny Miller at Birkdale, but the first of his three Open victories in 1979 was a rallying call that the Europeans were a rising force, a crusade close to his heart. Royal Lytham that year was pure adventure in which Ballesteros's stupendous powers of recovery knew no limits. It showed an inventive genius for shot-making but a calmer mood and more consistent vein surrounded his victory at St Andrews and his second at Lytham.

His insistence that The Open was the greatest of all championships was always added motivation; indeed, in 1984, the thought of winning at the Home of Golf was a double spur. His impromptu solo fandango that greeted his winning putt is part of The Open's folk lore but the delicate chip with which he settled the climax with a gallant Nick Price at Lytham in 1988 underlined a short game magic that was his trademark. His last round 65 was an impeccable display of golf.

SIR NICK FALDO
1987, 1990, 1992

Faldo's three victories in six years came in a concentrated period when he was arguably the best player in the world. In addition, he was runner-up in 1993, had five other top six finishes and lost a play-off for the US Open in 1988. He and Henry Cotton are the only British players to have won The Open three times since 1914.

All three successes showed all aspects of Faldo's many-sided game but his clear thinking always sensed the right time to attack and to defend. In the final round at Muirfield in 1987, he played every hole in par to break down the resistance of Paul Azinger, Faldo's opposing Ryder Cup captain in 2008.

Faldo's more spectacular front was revealed in his second victory at St Andrews in 1990 when he set a record (since broken) for the first 54 holes (199) and in 1992, when his 66, 64 set a record for the first 36 holes. He also jointly holds the record for the lowest aggregate for a runner-up (269) in 1993 at Sandwich. In 2009, he was the third Open champion to be knighted.

GREG NORMAN
1986, 1993

If success in major championships eluded him in the United States, Norman's two victories in The Open were most notable. In 1986 at Turnberry, first and third rounds of 74 showed the need for survival when bad weather destroyed many a hope.

His opening round left him four strokes behind the leader but a second round, 63, that included three putts on the 18th and equalled the lowest in the championship's history, transformed his fortunes. Always prepared to attack from the tee during the week when others were more fearful of the rough, a final 69 ensured a five stroke victory, the biggest since 1976. In the belief that victory should go to the best and most consistent player of the week, there was no other candidate.

In 1993 at Sandwich, Norman broke 70 in every round (something only two other champions have done since then) and set the record for the lowest final round by a winner with an immaculate 64. Norman lost a play-off in 1989 and, seeking to become the oldest winner at fifty-three, led after 63 holes at Birkdale in 2008 before finishing joint third.

TIGER WOODS
2000, 2005, 2006

It was a natural reaction to feel that something was missing when injury prevented Tiger Woods from playing in The Open in 2008. Nobody in the history of the oldest championship made a more explosive impact by his presence or by his golf. In 2000, he won by eight strokes with four rounds under 70 and without visiting a single bunker.

One explanation for winning again at St Andrews in 2005 by five strokes can be gleaned by his claim "I fell in love with the Old Course the first time I played it" but a year later on The Open's return to Hoylake, a change of scene brought the same result, his mastery of a fast-running links highlighting his great versatility. However, 2009 at Turnberry saw him fail to qualify for the final two rounds for the first time.

In his three victories, nine of his twelve rounds were under 70, clear indication of his inclination for strong front running but it is often overlooked that, in 1996, he equalled the lowest aggregate for an amateur. He is the only person to have won the Silver Medal for amateurs (1996) and the Gold Medal as a professional.

PADRAIG HARRINGTON
2007, 2008

Harrington's two Open victories could not have been more contrasting. The first at Carnoustie epitomised the pitfalls confronting a player when victory beckons especially on a notoriously difficult finish. His second at Birkdale used the mental strength derived from that first success to buoy him up sufficiently to pull away, like a true champion, when another close finish loomed. He played the last six holes at Birkdale in 4 under par to break the gridlock and win by four strokes, his second shots at the final two holes with a 5-wood and 5-iron being absolutely outstanding. Within a month, he became the first European to win the US PGA championship.

In 2007, Harrington led by a single stroke on the 72nd hole but visited Carnoustie's Barry Burn twice, eventually getting down in 2 for a 6 after two penalty drops. Moments later, Sergio Garcia failed narrowly with his four to win and it needed a play-off before a mightily relieved Harrington prevailed.

He proved a popular and worthy champion but never quite mounted a blow in his quest to win for a third year in succession at Turnberry.

Photography Credits

Photographs pages 6–7, 13, 14, 18–19, 28–29, 31, 42–43, 50–51, 32, 56 (bottom), 60–61, 64–65, 66, 68–69, 70, 72–73, 76–77, 94–95, 98–99, 106, 109, 110–111, 113, 118–119, 123, 124–125, 130–131, 138–139, 147, 148–149, 156–157, 166–167, 170, 171, 177 (top), 180–181, 182, 192–193, 197, 200–201, 206–107, 214–215, 222–223, 224, 225, 227 (top), 231, 232–233, 234–235, 240–241, 244–245, 246–247, 251, 256–257, 270–271, 276–277, 281, 285, and 296–297 by David Cannon.

Photographs pages 84–85, 144–145, 152–153, 228 (bottom), 230, 268–269, 289, 290–291, and 292–293 by Warren Little.

Photographs pages 32, 39, 85, 92–93, 112, 174–175, 202–203, and 226 by Steve Munday.

Photographs pages 58–59, 81, 107, 154, 155, 176, 248, and 284 by Ross Kinnaird.

Photographs pages 33, 158, 228 (top), 258–259 (bottom), 266, and 267 by Andrew Redington.

Photographs pages 162 (top), 177 (bottom), 286–287, and 288–289 by Stuart Franklin.

Photographs pages 41 and 229 by Richard Heathcote.

Photographs pages 80 and 82–83 by Harry How.

Photographs pages 162 (bottom) and 178–179 by Andy Lyons.

Photographs pages 172 and 262 by Simon Bruty.

Photographs pages 260 and 261 by Bob Martin.

Photograph page 38 by Paul Severn.

Photograph pages 86–87 by Steve Powell.

Photograph pages 88–89 by Howard Boylan.

Photograph page 218–219 by Don Morley.

Photograph pages 264–265 by Jamie Squire.

Photographs pages 30, 36–37, 45, 46 (top), 47, 53, 57, 73, 74, 79, 96, 108, 111, 116, 120, 122, 126, 128, 132, 134 (middle and bottom), 135, 136, 140, 141, 163, 165 (bottom), 168–169, 184–185, 190, 194 (top), 195, 218, 219 (bottom), 236, 242, 243, 250, 253, 259, 275, 279, 280 and 282 courtesy Getty Images Archive.

Photographs pages 23, 26, 46 (bottom), 48–49, 53 (bottom), 56 (top), 78, 90, 91, 142, 143, 150, 151, 160–161, 164, 165 (top), 186–187, 188, 189, 190 (bottom), 191, 194 (middle and bottom), 198, 208, 220–221, 227 (bottom), 252, 254–255, 272, and 283 courtesy Bob Thomas / Getty Images.

Photographs pages 84, 100, 110, 117, 121, 137, 258, 274, and 278 courtesy Popperfoto / Getty Images.

Photographs 102–103, 104–105, 114–115, 173, 199, and 216 courtesy Brian Morgan / Getty Images.

Photographs pages 8, 54–55, 62–63, 146, 196, and 204–205 courtesy *Sports Illustrated* / Getty Images.

Photograph pages 34–35 courtesy Time Life Pictures / Getty Images.

Photographs pages 40, 44, 134, and 238–239 courtesy *Golf Illustrated* / Bauer Media.

Photographs pages 10, 17, and 20 courtesy The R&A.

Photograph pages 212–213 courtesy the Royal Portrush Golf Club.

Photograph page 66 (bottom) courtesy RCAHMS.

Photograph page 297 (top) courtesy Peter Crabtree.